the treasury of
DOGS

Contributors

Wendy Boorer   Cecil Wimhurst

Barbara Woodhouse   Margaret Sheldon and

Barbara Lockwood

Octopus Books

Acknowledgements

The publishers would like to thank the following individuals and organizations for their kind permission to reproduce the pictures in this book:

Army Public Relations 116 bottom.
Australian News & Information Bureau 104, 105, 106.
Barnaby's Picture Library 46.
Canadian National Film Board 120–1.
Bruce Coleman 6, 16–17, 18, 28, 66 bottom left, 94, 122.
Colour Library International 31, 52 top right, 69, 71 top right, 72, 81, 82 centre, 100, 114.
Commissioner of Police 108.
Mary Evans Picture Library 101, 102 top and centre.
Fox Photos 48.
Michael Holford 9, 10, 11, 12, 14, 46, 58.
Keystone Press Agency 26, 70 top right, 82, 116 top.
Janis Leventhal 70 top left.
Barbara Lockwood 74, 76.
Frank H. Meads 49, 52 bottom, 57.
Dan O'Keefe 82 bottom.
Pierce 64 bottom.
Popperfoto 2, 20, 34–5, 36, 38, 39, 43, 68 centre, 75, 86, 87, 96.
Sheila Seale 63 bottom.
Spectrum Colour Library 13, 21, 22, 23, 25, 29, 33, 50–1, 55, 61 top, 63 top, 64, 68 top left, 70 bottom, 71 bottom, 80, 88–9, 95, 99, 107, 112, 119, 127, 128, 131.
Sport & General Press Agency endpapers, 54.
Syndication International 15, 24, 30, 37, 41, 45, 47, 56, 60, 65, 66 top, bottom right, 67 centre, bottom, 71 top left, 85, 102, 109, 110, 117, 118.
Sally Anne Thompson 8, 14, 40, 42, 52 top left, 59, 62, 67 top, 68 right and bottom, 77, 78–9, 81 bottom, 83, 84, 90–1, 92, 98, 124, 125, 126, 129, 130, 132, 133, 135.
Thurse 111.
Wembley Stadium 61 bottom.
Cecil Wimhurst 53, 115, 134.
Barbara Woodhouse 27, 32.

First published 1972 by
Octopus Books Limited,
59 Grosvenor Street, London W1

ISBN 7064 0009 7
© 1972 Octopus Books Limited
Reprinted 1975

Produced by Mandarin Publishers Limited
Toppan Building, Westlands Road,
Hong Kong

Printed in Hong Kong

Contents

Dogs and Man

WENDY BOORER

Wolves are still found in North America, Europe and Asia and are the domestic dog's closest relation.

When God created man and the beasts, He caused a great chasm to open between them. The dog, seeing the widening crack, ran forward and leapt over to join man, leaving the rest of the beasts on the other side. This legend is only one of many myths which seek to explain the especial relationship that exists between the human race and its canine followers. The dog was the first of the domesticated animals and the close association, which started in pre-history, has produced an animal today more responsive and receptive to his master than any other.

No one can state with certainty where and when this association began. Both wolves and jackals have been cited as the forerunners of the domestic dog. It is possible to cross both these species with the dog and produce hybrid offspring which are in their turn fertile. It was sometimes the practice, when sledge dogs were the only means of transport in the Arctic, for the Eskimos to stake out their bitches well away from the villages so that they might be mated to wolves. The resulting crossbreds, being both powerful and wary, often made good lead dogs for the sledge teams. In the past wolves were found much further south than they range now, and it is possible that the dog is descended from one of the smaller races of wolf such as the Indian wolf. The ease with which the dog and wolf can be bred together and the many behavioural similarities between the two indicate that the wolf today is the domestic dog's nearest wild relation.

We have to imagine the first tentative stages of co-operation between dog and man. At that time man was a nomadic hunter, not only forever moving in search of food but also himself the prey of the larger carnivores. When a good kill had been made the smell of the decaying offals and hides would attract scavenging packs of wild dogs. If food was abundant these might well be tolerated by man, and attracted by the easy pickings the packs of dogs would tend to follow the tribe's wanderings. People whose survival depends both on successful hunting and on avoiding the larger predatory animals have to be very familiar with the ways of both their intended victims and their possible enemies. In his awareness of animal behaviour primitive man was way ahead of his modern counterpart. It would not take long for these early hunters to realize that the pack of dogs round the camp could scent and hear possible game long before man became aware of its presence. At the same time the dogs, familiar with feeding on carrion close to man, would tend to drive off the smaller scavengers and protest volubly should anything larger and more dangerous approach. Man, realizing he could be protected and helped by the watchfulness of the dog, might then attempt to keep the pack near him by making sure that food was left for them.

The first great step towards domestication was taken when man and dog went hunting together. Bones of a large number of wild horses found in France suggest that at a very early stage in their relationship, man and packs of dogs combined to panic herds of grazing animals over the edge of cliffs. The resulting massacre more than sufficed for the needs of both. Dogs, too, would scent a wounded animal in hiding and hold it at bay until the hunters could arrive and complete the kill. Gradually, instead of following behind to share the spoils, dogs began to precede the hunters, finding and tracking the game.

As well as an early warning system and a hunting animal, man quickly found other uses for the dog. It is probable that young puppies at the weaning stage were taken into the camp and fed. These semi-tame animals would be a great deal more use than their wilder relatives outside and, being fatter and less stringy, they made a valuable addition to the larder when times were difficult. Dogs are still eaten in some parts of the world and there is no reason to doubt that this was one of the earliest uses of the first domesticated animal. Possibly, too, as the dog became tamer and could be safely handled, they had their uses as a source of warmth. Amongst primitive peoples today, dogs are still slung across the shoulder providing a certain amount of warmth and comfort against the chills of

7

dawn, and history records instances of dogs as hand or foot warmers in many parts of the world.

By the time man turned from hunting to keeping flocks and herds, the dog had become a necessity as a guard against predators and as a herding animal. The modern Border Collie, when penning sheep, shows by the slinking gait and the fixed stare that this herding skill derives from the instincts of a wild dog when hunting. The final dash and the kill are absent but nearly all the other movements of a sheepdog working sheep are also those of a predator stalking a prey. It was in harnessing and adapting this instinct in the dog that man made his greatest step forward in his use of the animal.

All these stages in domestication took place in the Middle Eastern countries and evidence suggests that by the time the dog reached Europe it was already a sheepdog. We have some idea of the appearance of some of these dogs from remains found by the Baltic Sea. In the late Stone Age the men who lived there built houses which stood on stilts in the water, and kept a small Spitz type dog with a wedge shaped head, prick ears and probably a curled bushy tail.

In the areas of the Middle East where domestication had originated, different types of dogs were already being bred with some care at a time when the more primitive peoples of the north were still at a much earlier stage of development. Egyptian pictures of 4000 BC show a greyhound type and a much larger, heavier animal with a blunter muzzle resembling a mastiff. Greyhounds hunt by sight rather than scent and use their superior speed to catch their victim. The hot still air of desert countries carries little scent but the visibility is often excellent, enabling the slightest movement to be seen at a great distance. Greyhounds are therefore splendidly adapted to hunt gazelle and other small antelope in what must be accepted as their country of origin.

Mastiffs appear on many early pictures, Babylonian and Assyrian as well as Egyptian. They are shown pulling down heavier game and as guard and watch dogs. They were also used for war, their necks being protected with massive collars. From their size, relative to the men leading them, they were obviously quite capable of killing a man and later accounts tell of large numbers of

A Border Collie racing to turn sheep back to the rest of the flock . . . the actions of a sheepdog are those of a wild dog stalking a prey, except that there is no final kill; man's domestication of the dog was a subtle adaptation of natural instinct.

8

A wall painting from the
Tomb of Ramasses VI in the Valley
of Kings, Egypt, showing long-legged
hounds with pointed ears rather like
the modern greyhound.

Two scenes from the Bear and Boar
Hunting Tapestry dating from the
Middle Ages which show huge
mastiffs in studded collars on the
point of attacking a wild boar
(left), and the hunt setting out
with the dogs on leads after the
friendly looking bears in the
background (right).

*Above, early Chinese ornaments.
'Lion Dogs' or 'Fo Dogs', the
ancestors of the modern Pekinese,
were carefully bred to resemble
dragons to drive away evil spirits,
and being very highly treasured
belonged only to those of royal blood.*

Above, a Spitz dog from Finland with the attractive wedge shaped head and prick ears of this breed. Stone Age remains of dogs like these have been found by the Baltic Sea, and the early Egyptians bred and kept small spitz-type dogs as pets – the mummified remains of these dogs decorated with ornate collars show that they were much loved by their owners.

such dogs appearing on the field of battle. Mastiffs like this are believed to have reached Britain with the Phoenician traders and were discovered here by the Roman invaders. What impressed the Romans was the size and ferocity of the British dogs. They were sent to Rome in some numbers to take part in the gladiatorial displays and their fame spread throughout the Roman Empire.

Before this however a number of different types of dog, some very similar to modern breeds, had appeared in the Middle East. The

Egyptians had a great talent for domesticating animals, and species which are wild today were kept by them in some numbers and were at least semi-tame. This skill with animals is also apparent in the pictures of their dogs, which were obviously bred with knowledge and care. By 3000 BC two kinds of greyhound appear, the second having large upright ears and looking very much like the modern Ibizan Hound. A little later the Saluki is shown with small pendent ears and slight feathering on the legs and tail. At the same time there were small,

Left, part of the frieze from the
Royal Palace of the Assyrian kings
at Ninevah showing the hounds used
for lion hunts being walked in the
park 612 BC.

Below, early illustration of a
mastiff; dogs of all descriptions from
a Bulldog to a Toy dog are pictured
behind him.

14

toy dogs of the Spitz type of which mummified remains have been found decorated with ivory bracelets and ornate collars, proof that they were highly regarded.

It is interesting in these early pictures to see the characteristics emerging which distinguish many of the modern breeds of dog. A tightly curled tail, such as is never found on a wild dog, appears on a small hunting breed looking like the modern Basenji. Long, low dogs with short legs call the Dachshund to mind. The small prick ear of the wild dog is changed to a larger upright bat ear on one type of greyhound and a small, folded rose ear on another.

The Middle Eastern peoples had no need for and never seem to have bred the hounds that hunt by scent, dogs with high domed foreheads and long pendent ears. These evolved in the cooler, milder climates further north where the thickness of the vegetation would prevent a greyhound seeing game, and where the humidity in the atmosphere produced good scenting conditions. These hounds were bred for good noses and the tenacity of purpose that would keep them on the trail of game until they had worn down the prey rather than overtaken it with speed. The early Greeks knew hounds of this type and used them for deer hunting. In general they did not exist in any numbers until the continent of Europe had achieved a stable and rich enough culture for the wealthy to indulge in a passion for hunting and the chase. Game laws of the Middle Ages reflect the importance of hunting to the nobility and it was probably at this time that the widest variety of scent hounds were kept and bred.

As well as these dogs of the chase, various types of spaniels are pictured. They are shown pointing game birds or flushing them into nets. They also found and put up birds for hawking and falconry, sports which reached their peak at this period of history.

Mention should also be made of toy dogs. The Egyptians kept diminutive animals as house pets. These could have had little practical use except as watch dogs and their early appearance in the history of the dog suggests that man has always felt the appeal of things in miniature. By 2000 BC the Chinese were also breeding several different types of dog with skill. This interest and expert knowledge about the dog continued in China almost up to the present day. Not only were careful accounts kept of kennel management and the appearance of new breeds but specific types were bred for meat, fur, hauling sledges, hunting etc. The greatest proof of Far Eastern skill in dog breeding, however, lies in the evidence of the small, flat-faced toy dogs that were produced there. Modern dog breeders are only too painfully aware of the pitfalls of miniaturization, which can often

Right, a Chinese Crested Toy dog. These are an ancient breed which are now however extinct in China and very rare elsewhere. They have practically no hair, and come in rather unusual colours, pink, blue or spotted.

produce skeletal abnormalities injurious to the dog's health. From the Far East however come the Pekinese, Pug and Shih Tzu, all relatively hardy, long-lived toy dogs which could only have been produced by skilled and knowledgeable breeding over the centuries.

Three types of dog existed in America before it was discovered by Europeans and were distinct from the wild dogs and wolves, the Eskimo dog, the Hair Indian dog and a smaller, Terrier-like dog found in the South. As already mentioned, the Eskimo dog may have been crossed with wolves, and it is probable that there have been dogs in the arctic regions of North America as long as men have lived there, since even primitive life would have been hard to sustain without the aid of the tough sledge dogs to provide transport. The Hair Indian dog was the North American Indians' only domesticated animal in pre-Columban times, and was used extensively for haulage up until the beginning of the nineteenth century when it disappeared completely. Some tribes used small types for food, while other tribes bred the animals specially for their hair for use in textiles. The small dog from the South was used exclusively for food and has also since disappeared.

Although the Coyote has never been considered as an ancestor of the domestic dog, it is possibly the most similar to it of all the wolves, and is still quite common on the North American prairies. Their behaviour was similar to wolves, although they are smaller and less predatory, until persecution by man forced them to become solitary hunters instead of hunting in packs. They have achieved considerable notoriety because of the range of their howl, and two coyotes singing together can sound like a whole pack.

A Coyote photographed in Alaska. They are only found in North America which makes it unlikely that they are a relation of the domestic dog in spite of the close resemblance, since dogs were first domesticated in the Middle East.

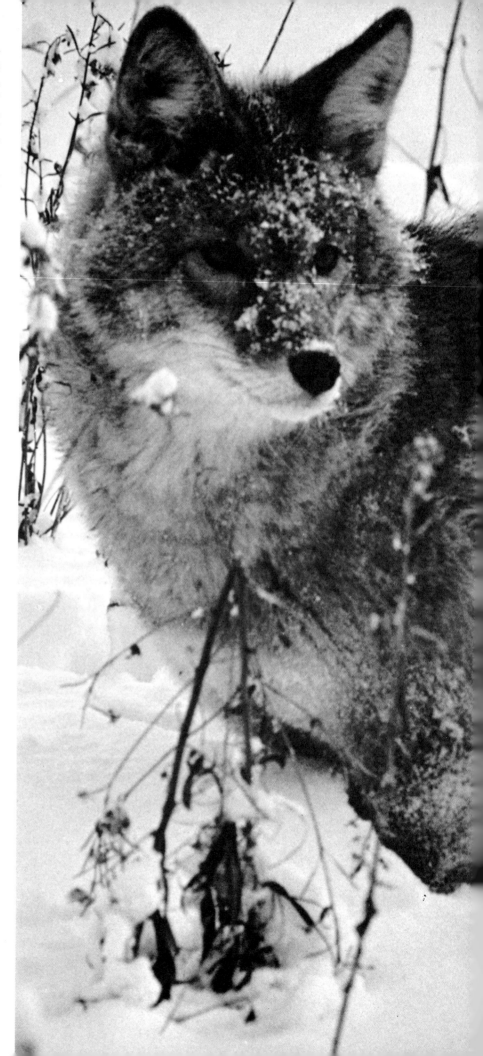

16

The Family Pet

BARBARA WOODHOUSE

Mongrels can be very intelligent and attractive pets with delightful characters . . . but there is usually an extra pleasure in owning a pedigree dog and taking an interest in a particular breed.

The choice of a dog for a family pet is a heavy responsibility for those who embark on it. So many people confuse the meaning of the word 'pet' with 'plaything', and choose a dog to satisfy the whims maybe of their children regardless of what is going to happen to the dog in its new environment. Under these circumstances when the children have tired of the dog, or the dog has tired of the children and shows it by nipping them, nobody seems to have any conscience about getting rid of the animal as soon as possible and embarking on some new foible. That is my interpretation of 'plaything'.

'Pet' however means something far deeper and implies involvement in the family circle. The new puppy or dog must be one that, ideally, the whole family wants; it must at any rate be the breed that appeals to the majority of the family, and it must be within their means to keep it in the way it should be kept.

Choosing the breed is most important. Mongrels can be perfectly charming devoted pets, but a thoroughbred always has that extra something which makes the family proud to own it, which is important, as well as possessing the hereditary characteristics that are known about the breed prior to purchase. A mongrel is always a gamble, especially one adopted from a lost dogs' home or from an appealing photograph in a newspaper. Most such dogs are wanderers by nature or they wouldn't be in lost dogs' homes. If such a dog is taken into the family it is always better to choose a bitch, as they settle more quickly and are more dependent on the family for all their pleasures. Few people seem to think enough in advance about the breed of dog to buy, and in particular about the length of the dog's hair. Mothers can become very annoyed at the amount of hair left around the house and on children's clothing, especially when the dog is casting its coat – which some dogs seem to do perpetually! They may also object to having to groom dogs such as Old English Sheepdogs or Afghans, who are liable to bring an enormous amount of mud into the house if not dried beforehand. Thus the choice of breed depends on how ready the

household members are to cope with the chores associated with their family pet. They might after thinking about it prefer to have a short-coated dog such as a Labrador, or an English Toy terrier, or a Poodle whose coat is never shed, although of course the clipping of the Poodle adds a certain amount to the cost of having one.

It must be very clear in the family's mind who is going to look after the dog before buying one. School children cannot carry out this task successfully, for during the greater part of the day the dog is left at home in their mother's care. Father may fancy, say, a Golden Retriever and see himself striding over the countryside with a gun and a perfectly trained gun dog to do the hard work. He may object to his wife and children spoiling the dog and making it soft when he wants a tough man's dog – for make no mistake, a family dog can become hopelessly spoilt by lack of discipline and be made useless as a working dog. If however the dog is only to be a family dog in name, and is in practice to be the Master's working dog, then there may be no problem.

Where a family can afford it, two dogs would be the ideal solution; one the well-trained working dog and the other a family pet willing to romp and be romped with, a role the Cavalier King Charles Spaniel would adore. These dogs are little trouble to own as they usually love everybody. Their coats need little grooming, a quick brush suffices, although sometimes the 'trousers' get a little soiled after functions have been performed, and have to be washed; but otherwise they are clean, cheap to feed, intelligent and good mixers with other dogs. They seem quite happy to stay indoors quietly, yet are always willing to go for a long walk. They don't appear to fret unduly when put into kennels, if the family is unable to take them on holiday. Exactly the opposite applies to breeds such as Alsatians and Great Danes, who become so utterly devoted to their families that they fret terribly if left behind. This is again a matter which must be faced before buying either of these breeds, as it means that their owners must plan their holidays to include taking

Above, 'We can't help it if we seem rather solemn, life is a very serious business, and anyway we are really rather appealing when we get together . . .'

From one extreme to another . . . it is important to decide when buying a dog whether you can cope with something as large as an Irish Wolfhound, let alone two, or whether something the size of this Terrier would not be easier to keep. In any case, it is a sure bet that he is making as much noise as the giants behind him.

the dog away wherever they go.

Terriers on the whole do not make ideal family pets since they are intolerant of children, especially West Highlands, Fox Terriers and Jack Russells. They look so adorable as puppies that many families have bought them on the spur of the moment, only to find that the dog's interest lies more in scents and the smell of rabbits than in playing games with the family. They are apt to disappear following a trail, to the intense frustration of the owner whose calls remain unanswered. Obedience can, of course, be remedied with adequate training, but few average families have the time or perhaps the money to train their dogs properly, and therefore it is probably better to choose a more amenable breed for the family dog.

The family pet should be an adaptable animal, it cannot expect to claim priority in every activity. It has to fit in and must therefore receive basic training in obedience right from the day it enters the household, usually at about 8 weeks old. Far too many people observe the view that you must wait until 6 months to train a dog. Quite categorically all puppies should learn to lie down and stay down, where put, from the very beginning, even if

only for a few minutes at a time. All its life a dog will have to stay put somewhere if it is to be a well behaved companion capable of accompanying the family wherever it goes.

Walking quietly on a lead follows on after the puppy has learnt to wear a collar without fuss, which should be put on the day the puppy arrives in the home. A young puppy of about 8 weeks old is very tractable and soon gets accustomed to anything new; if you wait until it is older it may shriek the place down or scratch its neck raw trying to remove the collar.

A puppy is quick at learning what it can get away with. For example it may lie on its back, all four feet in the air, and ready with needle-like teeth as an extra aid to disobedience. This is a trick most puppies are quick to adopt when trying to defeat weak owners. What people do not realize is that the act of lying on their backs and exposing their tummies is an instinct left over from the days when they were wild dogs running in packs, when they exposed their tummies to enemies. The law of nature respected this as an act of surrender and no other dog would attack them in this position. This attitude when adopted towards a human being also means that the

person is being treated as an enemy, which is not very flattering. So instead of saying 'how sweet' and rubbing its tummy, the puppy should immediately be made to sit or lie down in the normal position before it receives any praise or attention. If this is not done the owner is heading fast for further disobedience, and possibly at a later age a bite.

Too many members of a family all trying to train a puppy may confuse it, unless they use the same words of command and tones of voice. It is useless one member of the family shrieking with laughter when a puppy does wrong and another member spanking it for the same behaviour. Consistent training and daily practice for very short periods are the ideal way to bring up a family pet. A family dog must be a really happy dog; to be so it must have privacy, which means its own bed, chair or indoor kennel where it can escape from the family and where no-one must interfere with it. But it must also leave this sanctuary on command, if that command is sensible, which does not mean that children should be allowed to order it from its rest when it is tired and does not wish to play.

Far too many children maul dogs,

Above, Shetland Sheepdogs are very popular pets, their long silky coats, bright colours and intelligent, delicate faces are irresistible.

Left, the friendly and amusing Basset Hound, not perhaps the most intelligent or active of dogs, but extremely good natured, especially with children.

and forget that young puppies tire very easily. Mother may look upon the puppy as a plaything for the children so that she is free to get on with her chores. Then she may wonder why the puppy is listless and does not thrive. Puppies should seldom at an early age play for more than half an hour at a time, and should be left to sleep for the next two hours after which they should be put out to relieve themselves before being let free in the home. The early days of a puppy are much like those of a baby; food, short play times, and a lot of sleep make for healthy intelligent dogs.

Every dog can with understand-

ing, the right training and the right initial temperament, be made into a family pet providing the owners are right for that particular type and breed of dog. Few families have the time, knowledge or inclination to be dog experts; they just want a good pal, easy to look after, friendly, yet a good guard, and in robust health. No family should buy a trained guard dog unless it also has in that family a trained handler for such a dog. If the dog barks loudly at the approach of strangers that is as far as most family dogs should go; it is sufficient deterrent for most criminals. Always buy a bold puppy, shy ones are potential biters.

A seven-week-old St Bernard puppy has a very knowing look on his face as he plays at being an Alpine rescue dog . . . the only snag is that he keeps tripping over the barrel.

Opposite, Springer Spaniels make enchanting pets, although they are really working dogs.

Here is a list of some breeds which I think make good family pets.

Small Breeds
Poodles. English Toy Terriers. King Charles Spaniels. Cavalier King Charles Spaniels. Boston Terriers. Pugs. French Bulldogs. Griffons. Corgis, if trained early. Dachshunds. Spaniels of all types, with the exception of the Red Cocker whose temperament in England has deteriorated over the years. Schipperkes. Beagles are happy, tolerant family dogs, but are not easily trained and are rather too interested in outdoor scents to be ideal family pets.

Medium Breeds

Labradors of the smaller variety, bitches being better than dogs. Golden Retrievers. Weinmaraners. Alsatians with good temperaments. English Setters and Gordon Setters. Boxers. Bearded Collies, but not Border Collies which are working dogs and not happy as family pets. Basset Hounds, if you don't mind an indolent, good natured, rather dim dog as far as obedience training goes. They do not mind children at all, but prefer to keep their noses to the ground when out walking; in my opinion more funny than fun.

Large Breeds

St Bernards. New Foundlands. Great Danes. An important point about the latter: never forget that a Great Dane must have early training in implicit obedience. It needs a lot of rest, vast amounts of calcium and nourishing food with vitamins to keep it healthy in its staggering rate of growth (this applies to all big breeds) and no exercise except what it wishes to indulge in for the first six months of its life.

Because I have mentioned only a few of the 300 breeds of well-known dogs it doesn't mean that I condemn the rest. It means that, having trained over 13,000 dogs with their owners, I have found these breeds to be on the whole good mixers with humans and with other dogs. They are trainable – or too indolent to be very disobedient – and therefore seem happy as family pets. There are perfect and hopeless dogs in every breed. Try to get an expert to help you choose the right puppy for your family conditions.

Early Days in the Family Circle

The first few days with the family may be disturbing for both puppy and household. If there are youngsters in the family the novelty of a new pet will be terrific. They will all want to hold it, play with it, feed it, pet it and have it for themselves. Parents will have to be very firm, very tactful and very sympathetic to the puppy's needs. When there are children it is sometimes better to get an older dog which is accustomed to them, reasonably well behaved and clean in its habits, rather than a very young puppy.

A puppy often puddles all over the place through fear and a feeling of insecurity and lack of warmth. It is not accustomed to being carried about often very awkwardly by inexperienced people. (The correct way to hold a puppy is with the

25

Left, Barbara Woodhouse's Junia, star of over a hundred films, practising her first moves at seven weeks old.

Below, the visitors on one of Mrs Woodhouse's training week-ends come in every shape, size and colour, and by the end of the week-end they are nearly always doing what they are told.

middle finger between its front paws and the other fingers and thumb supporting its legs, with its back legs resting on the inside of the owner's elbow or hip.) Never let a puppy's body hang down unsupported. It can momentarily be lifted up by the scruff or loose skin on the back of its neck when very young, but as it gets older this is not a good idea. Too much carrying about is bad for puppies, as is too much running about. If they are to grow up with straight legs they must have adequate rest.

Large breeds should not be taken for actual walks until about six months old; short playtimes in the garden suffice. Riding in cars from an early age accustoms puppies to the motion of the car and they are then unlikely to be car sick. They should never be allowed in the front seat where they are a potential danger to themselves and to the driver in an emergency. The longer they are in the car, even if it is stationary in your yard, the less likely they are to be car sick, since they get to know the car as a safe place, especially if their own cushion or blanket is put on the back seat. Bad drivers are the cause of many dogs being car sick, so if the dog is unwell drive more smoothly. Remember it is extremely dangerous to leave dogs in a car in hot weather without adequate shade and air. Dogs have died through thoughtless owners leaving them shut up in cars.

In these days of little domestic help, and dog sitters difficult to get, you may have to take the dog with

you if you are going out for a long day. Some of your friends may welcome your dog, and if it is properly trained (especially house trained) it is a welcome guest. But others may dislike dogs, or are allergic to them, or have such beautiful houses that pawmarks or hairs are not wanted, and the only way you can take your dog along on such a visit is to have it so well-behaved that you can leave it in your car with any easy mind, certain that it will not chew the upholstery or nearly go mad panicking when left alone. All this comes from early training to lie down and stay down and relax.

If the family pet belongs to a reasonably disciplined family one usually finds a confident and happy dog. If the children are fiends, and the father yells at everyone, or the mother tends to burst into tears or smacks the children as an alternative, the dog tends to be mixed up. Dogs are very sensitive to atmosphere. Training should be done by the calmest member of the family.

Right, two proud Pekinese with a West Highland White Terrier.

Weinmariners make equally good pets or gun dogs and have a very unusual coat colour – it is a soft mushroom or silver grey, and the eyes are amber coloured.

28

A magnificent Afghan Hound
showing off his long silky coat as he
overtops his young mistress. Dogs
like these need a lot of care and
attention as well as regular exercise.

Right, the responsibilities of dog
ownership must be remembered before
one succumbs to the irresistible
charm of puppies like this one . . .

Never should any puppy – or dog for that matter – be taken to bed by any member of the family; it is unhealthy, habit forming and disturbs both dog and person. A puppy should stay put in its own allotted bed.

One hears all sorts of theories, good and bad, about teaching a puppy tricks. If he likes being clever what possible harm can there be in enlarging his repertoire? I well remember as a youngster watching *Rin Tin Tin* and coming home from the local cinema to teach my Alsatian some of the tricks I'd seen that dog star perform. Then getting my school pals to come and watch my dog's performance. The dog loved being clever and our relationship deepened considerably; he used to race around all my friends when they clapped as if to say 'Aren't I clever?' I did not give him tit-bits as reward because I think feeding dogs between meals is bad for their digestion; it also makes a dog think it must have a reward every time it is clever. I believe the owner's pleasure is enough reward for a beloved dog.

Left, Cavalier King Charles Spaniels make ideal family pets and are very popular in Britain, although they are not yet recognized by the American Kennel Club. These Blenheims belonging to Mrs Woodhouse are experienced performers in films.

The craze for poodles is past its height but they are still one of the most popular pets due to their intelligence and companionship. This one has been clipped for showing.

Feeding

Everyone has different ideas on how a dog should be fed. The breeder has his ideas, your vet may have different ones. The local animal lover may give her theories, and if you watch television the commercials are put out so well that you might be persuaded to rush out and buy 'Champy Beans' in response to a powerful advertisement.

One wonders how one's ancestors ever fed their dogs in their 'utter ignorance' of what a dog needs. When I was a child our dogs had chicken carcasses thrown to them, and scraps from the table were the main diet of our Alsatian, Fox Terrier and Cocker Spaniel. These dogs always looked extremely fit and lived to a ripe old age. Nowadays no one in their senses would give

Sealyham Terriers were bred as badger dogs but they make excellent pets since they have great charm and a distinct sense of humour.

chicken bones to dogs, for we know that the sharp bones might stick in its throat, or perforate its intestine.

Some people claim that large dogs need up to 6 lbs of meat a day, and it has been said that $2\frac{1}{2}$ ozs of food is necessary per lb of the dog's weight, which I reckon for a large dog of about 150 lbs in weight would work out at 23 lbs of food a day! Perhaps this calculation makes sense for a very young puppy, but as the dog grows up even the biggest one does not need more than 2 lbs of meat daily.

People feed their pets vast quantities of tinned dog food these days, good quality butcher's meat being far too expensive for the average family pet. Some of these tinned foods are excellent, others are not so good. The high fat content of some is inclined to give the dogs diarrhoea, so choose a good brand. It stands to reason that tinned foods must contain some of the cheaper types of meat or they could not be produced at 'pet' prices. Most people vary their pet's diet. Feeding a puppy is almost the same as feeding a baby. In fact many puppies are fed on cereals made for babies. With the cost of everything perpetually

rising, fish is often a cheap change of diet.

When you buy a puppy the breeder usually supplies a diet sheet which should be followed, if possible, for at least a week. Violent changes of diet upset the puppy's digestion. After that you must use your own commonsense or buy a book, or get advice from another dog owner. The condition of the puppy will prove whether you are feeding it correctly. Above all, remember that a puppy needs added vitamins, calcium and bone meal in whatever diet you choose.

I often hear people boast that they never feed their dog at mealtimes, which I am sure is a very commendable thing. But I also think that if the dog is in the dining room when a meal is being eaten the smell of the food must make its saliva run, which is what happens when the dog's system signals that it is going to get something to eat, and therefore it might be better for the dog to be banished from the dining room, or alternatively be given his own meal at the same time.

I never make rules about what people should or should not do with their dogs except to say never let

Two of the largest breeds of dog. Left, an Irish Wolfhound is the mascot of the Irish Guards and shows off his enormous size as he stands up to greet his handler. Right, a proud and imposing family of Champion Great Danes. It is so easy to fall for the puppies of dogs like these without being fully aware of the size they will eventually reach and the amount of exercise and food they will need.

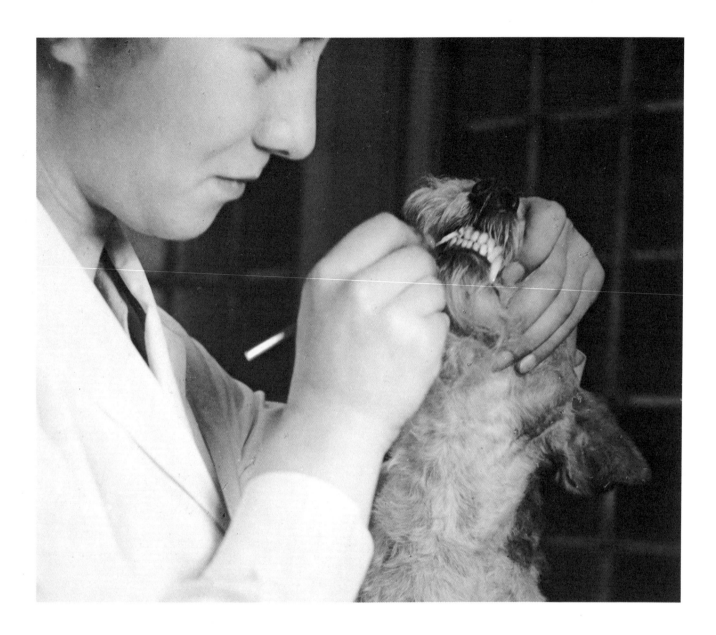

your dog be a nuisance or a danger to anyone, and above all, never let your dog over-eat or get fat. A fat dog is liable to kidney and heart trouble; it is an ugly sight and not a credit to its owner; its life expectancy is shortened and I feel that any family which lets its pet get into this unhealthy condition through over-feeding are not dog lovers in the true sense of the word. I know that in some cases it is difficult to keep a dog slim because children are forever sucking, chewing or eating something, and many such tit-bits find their way into the mouth of the family pet especially if it has been taught to beg, which melts even the hardest heart. If it is to keep fit and well, food of any sort must be confined to what it really needs for its health.

Myths and facts about dog health

So many things, good and bad, are believed about dogs without foundation. In fact many people are scared to own one for fear it may bring disease to their family. They worry that dogs carry TB, which of course under certain circumstances they do, but those circumstances are now so rare they can be ignored. In the old days cattle were the chief source of TB, either through their milk or meat, and when slaughtered the meat was sold for animal consumption. Thus there was a real risk of a dog getting TB and being a source of infection. Nowadays, with TB practically eliminated, I think no one need worry. What is necessary where dogs are concerned is to be sure they do not have tapeworms, for

their presence can be a source of danger to humans causing a particularly nasty form of paralysis. Most people have their dogs wormed by their vet, and in any case tapeworms are not very common in pedigree dogs because breeders worm the dams and the puppies before selling them to their new homes. If however a puppy is thin, has dull eyes and is listless, it is wise to consult your vet about the possibility of all worms.

The entire family should be taught never to kiss a dog on the mouth, or let the dog lick the children's faces. I always taught my puppies the command 'no lick', and would kiss them behind the ear where there can be no possible danger of anything being passed from dog to human. Again, once proper worming

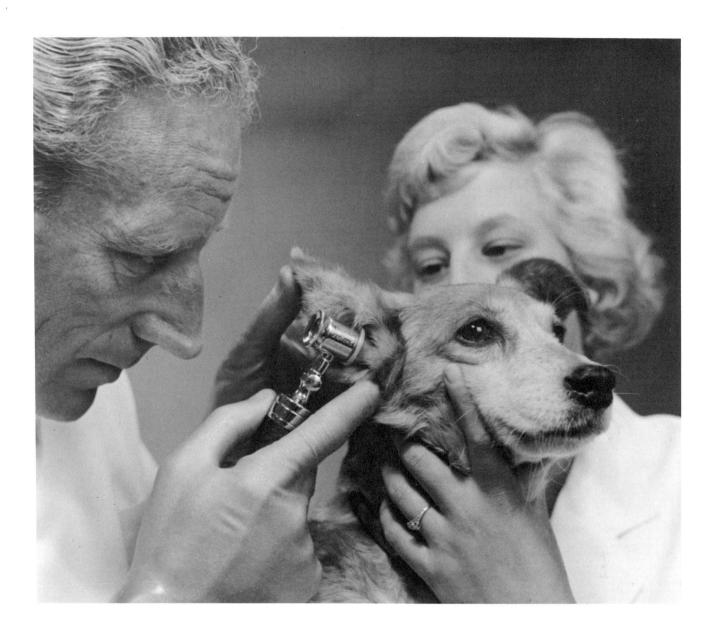

has been carried out the risk of any infection is negligible. Dogs should be kept clean and free from fleas and lice by using powders or bathing with proprietary dog soaps. Some dogs may eat manure because their diet lacks something they need, like trace elements. On being given sufficient minerals etc. they cease this unpleasant habit.

Some people say that they hate dogs because they smell. This can of course be true if the dog is kept in dirty places and never bathed. But I am sure no family pet would be like this. What may cause offence is bad breath, which comes from bad teeth that need scaling. Mothers send their children to the dentist but fail to have the vet examine their dog's teeth, which require scaling at about three-monthly intervals. To

carry out this service the dog must be trained from early days to have its mouth opened without fuss or biting, something few people remember until too late. Without training there is usually an almighty struggle and eventually the vet has to give the dog a general anaesthetic before being able to scrape its teeth. Remember, that if ever your dog is ill and requires to have pills it must allow its mouth to be opened: so start training early.

What frightens a dog most is tenseness in the owner. When anything has to be done the owner should try to relax, or the dog will pick up the tense atmosphere and trouble is the result. Never send the dog to the vet with a child. Send the calmest adult in the family or better still get the vet to call at the house.

It's a dog's life . . . but clean teeth and clean ears are very important, and both should be attended to regularly.

The dog will be happier in its own surroundings, and there is always a risk that a puppy may pick up some disease when it visits a vet's surgery. Many families don't budget for the dog being ill and forget to insure against this happening. They also forget to make their gardens safe so that the dog cannot get out and cause an accident or be killed. They also don't think about their dog barking or howling when they leave it alone in the home, which can cause much friction with the neighbours.

Few people train their dogs to relieve themselves at set times, so causing annoyance to people by allowing their dogs to foul pavements or sidewalks and laying themselves open to fines for allowing such behaviour. Yet I trained my dog to perform either of her personal functions on my word of command and it was not a difficult thing to teach. Mothers train their babies to be regular, yet never dream of doing the same thing with their puppies.

The puppy is not considered to have that amount of intelligence. Little do they know what heights of intelligence a dog can reach if the family takes the time and trouble to teach it. People are inclined to sneer if one claims that dogs can understand nearly every word we say, but I know it can be true. In fact they can understand every thought let alone words, for they have an acute telepathic sense and the spoken word becomes unnecessary. When I hear some humans nagging away I wish telepathy were used more often in human relationships!

The Family Pet versus the Show Dog

What is the difference between the family pet and the show dog or working dog? There can be a vast difference or there need be no difference. But it is not often the family pet which gets high honours in the show ring, for the family hasn't time to spend at shows. The

training is very different; the dog always has to look alert in the show ring and the family dog is so used to hustle and bustle that the show ring wouldn't make it look alert, probably just bored.

Usually the family pet is not the most expensive puppy in the litter and may have minor faults or be mismarked, like a merle Great Dane which is not permitted to be shown under English Kennel Club rules. A mismarked dog can be of superb conformation and outstanding intelligence, when it can be trained for the Obedience Ring at shows and win high honours. But there again it takes endless time and few family pets get this training where there are children in the family. Border Collies are often bought to train for Obedience, and are also kept as family pets which I think very sad. In my opinion a Border Collier is a dog that should be kept on a farm, working sheep or cattle and thereby fulfilling its destiny. I meet many

'You have to mix in with all sorts
in a large family . . .'

Left, a beautiful New Foundland –
another breed recommended by the
author as being easy to train and
which makes a happy family pet.

of these dogs, hopelessly mixed up and trying to chase cars or bicycles.

There are plenty of Exemption shows, usually run for charity, where classes are put on for the dog with the most beautiful eyes or longest tail, and this is where the family pet comes into its own, although I have seen tiny children burst into tears when their dog hasn't won a prize. Personally I don't think dogs like being shown, and no dog likes being stared at. As a child my Mother taught me it was rude to stare at anyone; why is it less rude to stare at our four-footed friends?

A dog should be a complete member of the family, its rights and privileges should have the same consideration as any other member of the family within reason. The reward of owning a well-behaved, loving and intelligent dog is beyond measure. Those who have owned such a dog are truly blessed. In these circumstances the words 'family pet' can be dropped, for the dog has indeed become one of the family.

A Golden Retriever (left), and a Pyrenean Mountain Dog.

43

Hounds and Hunting Dogs

C. G. E. WIMHURST

Most authorities agree that the immediate ancestor of the dog was a wolf and it is interesting to speculate how pre-historic men first established a working relationship with these fierce and shaggy creatures. One thing is certain – there was no sentiment on either side, and in a world where the only law was eat or be eaten, the partnership survived because co-operation resulted in a full larder in the cave and a satisfying tightness in the belly of the wolfdog.

It is to St Hubert that credit must go for originating the fine hounds which have spread into most parts of the world. The Saint, in his early days, was a dissolute young nobleman who placed hunting before his religious duties, and legend has it that a stag emerged from a thicket bearing a fiery cross between its antlers, a sight which terrified the hounds and greatly surprised Hubert. The stag remonstrated with the young man, reproved him for hunting on a Good Friday, and threatened him with hellfire unless he improved his ways. This so impressed the young nobleman that he gave up his wild life and founded the Abbey of St Hubert in the Ardennes. Whatever the truth of

his conversion, he continued to breed his hounds until he died in AD 727. His white and black and tan hounds were strong and possessed great powers of scent, and the monks of St Hubert's Abbey carried on the strain for many centuries after his death.

In France hunting has always been considered as an art, and the science of hound breeding was known there many years before attempts at selective breeding were made in other parts of the world. William the Conqueror brought his hunting hounds to England in 1066, and the Norman knights hunted stags, since hares, the traditional English quarry, were not considered worthy of their attention. Their hounds were big, strong animals of the St Hubert strains, which were capable of pulling down the strongest stag, and were either black and tan or pure white. The latter were known as Talbots, now only remembered by the occasional name board hanging from the door of a

An outstanding Foxhound of the Eridge Hunt.

country hotel. As time passed, the original St Hubert strains were interbred with other hounds, and animals with shorter legs became the more usual type. These, although losing something in speed to the original Norman hounds, still retained the good nose and melodious voice of their ancestors.

However, in those days of poor communications hounds varied a great deal in type and a book written in the fifteenth century, attributed to Edward Duke of York, provides useful information concerning the way in which all kinds of hounds hunted boars, badgers, foxes, otters, wolves and hares. It would appear that the hounds and their quarry were a very mixed bag and anything that moved was considered worthy of the chase.

Hunting was unrestricted in England until King Canute introduced severe game laws, which the Con-queror then enforced with increasingly savage penalties. It was made illegal for commoners to own any sort of hound, although a sheepdog or a small animal could be kept. Killing a deer was punished by death or mutilation, and the forest wardens made sure that large dogs were incapable of hunting by striking off the first three toes of one forefoot. King John added further regulations, since hare, and particularly deer hunting, were the chief occupations of the nobility, and it was during his reign that otter hunting also became a popular sport. Stag hunting declined during the seventeenth century when Cromwell broke up the great deer parks, forcing the country gentlemen to seek other quarry. Thus the fox ceased to be regarded as vermin which was killed by any means at hand and the 'little red rascal' has survived to this day as a worthy, clever and fast quarry which, more often than not, lives to run another day. Certainly, by the reign of Queen Anne fox hunting was general all over Britain.

The Crown Colonies of Virginia and Maryland in America were mainly settled by emigrants from England who lived as far as possible the lives of English gentlemen, enjoying hunting and the other field sports so common in their homeland. It is not surprising, therefore, that the first foxhounds imported into America in 1650 came to Virginia. There was an abundance of game in both colonies and the hounds hunted many different animals; the racoon, for instance, provided excellent sport. In due course other hounds were brought from England and breeding flourished, although the types were many and varied in different parts of the country. It is interesting to note that the red fox was imported specially for hunting and found the country so much to its liking that it soon rivalled the native grey fox in numbers.

George Washington was an enthusiastic hound breeder and the Marquis de Lafayette sent him several French hounds with which to improve his stock. There are no records to show if breeding operations were successful and all trace of the progeny was lost, since many breeders were trying to establish strains which would combine scenting ability with persistence and stamina. Dozens of strains were produced, and the more famous ones such as the

Walker hounds, and the Triggs and Birdsongs were named after their breeders. The ancestor of the Coonhound was the Virginian black and tan dog, but there is strong reason to believe that there is more than a little bloodhound in this accurate and specialized hunting dog.

Now, after centuries of breeding with only one object in view – the mental and physical suitability of the hound for its work – there are few, if any animals so perfect in structure as the modern foxhound bred in Britain and the United States. They are exported to most of the civilized countries of the world, and hunt such unlikely quarries as

The hounds with the Whip and Master of the Heythrop setting out for wooded country after the meet.

Right, hare hunting is one of the oldest sports in the world and the harrier is one of the oldest breeds – these hounds from the Derbyshire Peaks are very like Foxhounds but slightly smaller.

Foxhounds are pack animals and are not so dependent on human companionship as other dogs. It is not possible to make pets of them, but the huntsman knows all his hounds intimately and they obey and understand him as well as any other highly trained dog.

50

Far left, two Rhodesian Ridgebacks. These hounds are still used for big game hunting in Africa and are now becoming increasingly popular in Britain and America as family dogs.

Left, the popular Afghan hound.

Bottom, a pack of Otterhounds; note the two shaggy dogs in the middle of the foxhounds; they are the ancient type of Otterhound and are seldom seen today.

Below, New Forest Buckhounds are larger and sturdier types of Foxhound trained to hunt deer.

jackals in places where the red fox does not live.

However, strict training is necessary to counteract their natural hunting instincts. Left to themselves hounds will hunt anything which takes their fancy and they have to be trained to follow the chosen quarry. Foxhounds are taught to ignore other scents and follow the trail of the fox no matter how tempting the scent left by other animals. No rioting is allowed, and instant obedience to the huntsman is essential. It must be remembered that hounds are not so dependent upon human companionship as other dogs. They are pack animals, and the same responses to men are neither found nor desired as in a pet dog living in the house, so any form of training other than that connected with their work in the field is a waste of time.

It is not possible for men to understand just how much hounds depend upon their sense of smell. Scent is the minute particles of matter which are deposited all the time by every living creature, whether moving or still, and is quite out of their control. Scent is left upon grass, hard roads, plants or trees and on snow and ice. It will be deposited on water but will be moved swiftly away by the current. It can be carried by the wind and hang in the air so that a hound can follow it breast high. A damp atmosphere is favourable to scent, but a slight wind on a dry day will quickly cause it to evaporate, and in a strong wind it will dissipate very quickly indeed. A scent over seven hours old is stale, although a bloodhound has been known successfully to complete a trail many hours colder.

Foxhound puppies are not reared in kennels but sent out to 'walkers' – volunteers who will take a puppy or two and look after them until the age of six months. This ensures that the pups get a good start in life and receive the individual attention which would not be possible in hunt kennels. Furthermore, they learn to care for and trust humans. It is never easy to part with a puppy

53

which has been one of the family, but there is always another puppy to look forward to.

When they return to the kennels puppies are first taught to recognize their names and conform to kennel discipline. After this the young hound is coupled to an older hound which already knows the words of command and will drag the puppy with him, thus enabling the novice quickly to connect the command with the action. Further training is given until the young hounds can be trusted not to pursue sheep, cattle or any other domestic animals. Exercise is important to build up stamina and accustom them to horses, traffic and any obstacles they might find when fully fledged members of the pack. A whole book could be written on the subject of training and entering foxhounds, but enough has been written to indicate the main outlines.

In Britain Foxhounds are not shown at dog shows held under Kennel Club rules, but there are annual shows recognized by the Kennel Club of which the most important is the one at Peterborough. Other annual events are held at Aldershot and Honiton while the Great Yorkshire show caters for the North.

The American Foxhound is very similar to the English type and both stand some 23–25 inches at the shoulder. The American hound is decidedly leggier but it has been bred to the same high standards as his British cousin.

The Beagle is a small, active hound with a long history and it has varied in size and use over the centuries. Queen Elizabeth I possessed a number of them, said to be small enough to be packed into a saddle bag and carried on a horse. Beagles are followed on foot while hunting hares and they are very keen and persistent hounds. At one time a beagle was used to find hares for greyhounds to course. The first beagles to arrive in the United States in 1870 were used to hunt

Right, Bloodhounds have the finest noses of all hounds and are, as their sad and solemn faces suggest, very friendly and good natured dogs.

Below, Beagles off to the first draw. They are followed on foot while hunting hares and the sport is becoming increasingly popular in Britain, although not yet so well attended nor as spectacular as fox hunting.

rabbits and hares and some packs were sent after foxes – an experiment which was not repeated since the little hounds were not fast enough.

They are not always used as hunting dogs, and are quite capable of settling in with the family as a pet. Some breeders are trying to produce a small type which will be even more suitable as a house dog. The reduction in size would certainly take it out of the hunting world and the project has not found favour with hunting folk. However, the popularity of the beagle as a pet continues to grow.

It is sometimes thought that the Bloodhound, by reason of its name, is a savage creature which leaps with open jaws upon its quarry at the end of the trail. Nothing could be further from the truth – this large and solemn looking dog is a good

natured animal which is so delighted at coming up with the man he has been following that he puts his forefeet on his shoulders and wipes a long, moist tongue round his face in friendly greeting. For this reason they are being superceded by Alsatians as police dogs, although they are still used extensively in America for following and finding missing people. Descended from the hounds of St Hubert, he has the finest nose of all hounds and will follow a cold line successfully long after other breeds have given up.

Training is started at an early age and the puppy's first lessons are taught as a game. The trainer hides behind a tree or other object and waits until the pup notices his absence. The little fellow will look all round and then put his nose to the ground and follow the trail,

Above, a pack of Bloodhounds setting off to follow a laid trail or 'drag', which is a substitute for a fox. The field usually follows Foxhounds on a drag hunt in areas where foxes are scarce, and can have a very good run. Bloodhounds being hunted is a rare sight these days.

Right, off for a day's hunting with a pack of Basset Hounds . . . these comical looking dogs are usually thought of as house dogs, but they have excellent noses and cover the ground surprisingly thoroughly, tiring the hare out by persistence rather than overtaking it with speed.

56

receiving much praise and patting when he finds his master. This is repeated time after time until the game turns into a lesson; the puppy is held while the trainer walks away out of sight, and when released, soon puts his nose to the ground and follows the line until he finds his trainer. The next step is to teach him to take the scent and follow a trail from the smeller, which is an article of clothing or anything else holding the scent of his quarry. Patience is needed at this stage but the puppy will connect the smeller with the scent on the ground after several lessons and from then on it is a matter of practice.

The friendly and somewhat comical-looking Basset Hound is also descended from the St Hubert Hound, although he only arrived in England just over a century ago. Like the beagle his job is to hunt the

hare, the field following on foot at a pace which allows time to observe the fine nose work as the pack follow every twist and turn of their elusive quarry. The Basset has the loveliest hound music of all the breeds and his melodious deep voice echoing from the hills is something to remember. Quite apart from hunting, the Basset makes an excellent house dog and has been increasing in popularity in Britain and the United States; he has also been known to excel as a show dog and in obedience contests. Since the Second World War the English Basset Hound – a slightly straighter and longer legged version of the French hound – has been used by all Basset Hunts in England except one, since they are more capable of hunting all day without tiring.

Hare hunting is certainly one of the oldest sports in the world and

the Harrier is a very ancient breed although it has varied in form over the years. It is larger than the Beagle but smaller than the Foxhound to which it is related and which it resembles very closely. The first recorded pack in England was the Penistone which was founded in the thirteenth century and continued in existence for the next five centuries. In those days the hunt was followed on foot and not on horseback as today; modern harriers are bigger and faster and some packs hunt foxes as well as hares. They were taken to America by the early settlers and used for both sports but the hare is now the chief quarry although some packs are used for drag hunts.

Otter hunting has never been so popular in Britain as the pursuit of deer, foxes and hares, but it is an ancient sport and it is recorded that

Henry II of England owned several packs. It is not known what form his hounds took, and the old type of shaggy hound is now seldom seen. Its origin is unknown but it has been said that spaniels, Airedale terriers, bulldogs and greyhounds were all part of its make-up, and possibly bloodhounds as well as it has a very sensitive nose indeed. There is only one pure bred pack left in Britain, as most of the hunts use foxhounds, although there are some packs with an odd couple of Otterhounds in them. Lack of breeding stock would seem to indicate that this fine old hound is on the way out. They were taken to America sometime at the end of the last century but the breed has never been popular there and few hunting packs were formed. Some specimens are seen at shows but it is not likely that registrations will increase much in the future.

To America must be given the whole credit for evolving the Black and Tan Coonhound, or 'Cooner' as he is known for short, used for hunting the racoon. His immediate ancestor is the Virginian Foxhound, but he can also trace his lineage back through the bloodhound to the hounds of St Hubert and to the Talbot of William the Conqueror. The hunting of the racoon is a very specialized sport since it takes place at night. The Coonhound follows the scent of the coon on the ground and this animal sooner or later seeks refuge in a tree – it is very often later since the coon hunt may take several hours before the quarry is treed. The hound must, therefore, show great persistence in following the line. Once the coon has taken to the tree, the Coonhound will stand underneath and give his deep, typical tree bark, and the hunters can then move in for the kill.

The Coonhound is purely a working dog and is almost never kept as a pet or companion. Indeed, as in the case of most hounds, excessive domestication would dull his natural instinct for hunting and another worker would be lost to the world!

A hunter of bigger game is the Rhodesian Ridgeback. This is a large hound of 24–27 inches at the withers and is distinguished by a ridge of hair growing in the opposite direction to the rest of the coat. It is thought that the breed originated from a native hunting dog crossed with a bloodhound, and it has even been suggested that some lion blood was introduced. This theory is interesting but impossible, and springs from the nature of the Ridgeback's work which is to hunt lion and hold it up by pretending to attack until the hunter can get in a shot. There are no lions in Britain or America but the hounds are fine, intelligent animals and are finding favour in both countries as companion dogs.

One of the most versatile of hounds, the Norwegian Elkhound, is virtually the same as it was over 6000 years ago, and it is certainly one of the oldest breeds in the world. It has worked as a herding dog, a guard dog, a companion dog to the family and a hunter of elk. Working

in pairs, the Elkhounds would pick up the scent of one of these huge animals and trail it until it turned at bay. The hounds would attack, dodging the flailing hooves of the animal until the hunters arrived. It was, and is, the supreme utility dog of Norway, and, due to its intelligent and attractive appearance, appears to be increasing in popularity in Britain and America.

A hound which is no longer used for its original purpose in Britain and the United States is the Dachshund, which in its native Germany is used, as its name implies, to hunt badgers. In this it is suited physically since its powerful body, supported on short, strong legs, enables it to enter the badger's earth and force a way through the tunnels until he can come to grips with the quarry. It is the only hound which goes to earth in the manner of a terrier, but there is no proof that any terrier blood was used in its make-up.

The Standard type measure some 10 inches at the shoulder and are found in three variations of coat: Smooth, Long haired, and Wire haired. There are miniatures in all three which are very popular indeed. Dachshunds are intelligent, very affectionate and loyal and have a sense of humour. The opportunity to hunt badgers may be limited but a Dachshund in the house more than makes up for the loss of sport, and there is no better companion in either town or country.

The only hound in the world which has no voice is the little Basenji, the barkless dog of the Congo. Not entirely dumb, it can make a sound like a canine yodel, but bark – never. Extremely intelligent, with a wrinkled forehead and bright eyes, it is a medium sized, square dog with a very short coat chestnut red, black and tan or black in colour. The breed came to England in 1936 and the first imports to the United States arrived in 1940–1. Good tempered and affectionate,

the Basenji has made firm friends in both countries.

The gaze hounds, or the hounds which hunt by sight, are quite different in appearance from the heavier hounds which hunt by scent. The greyhound family share many basic characteristics both mental and physical. They are all finely triggered, slim and long-legged, and very fast. Further, they all derived from the hunting dogs of ancient Egypt and are probably one of the oldest breeds in the world.

Left, a rare treat for these handsome Dachshunds which probably arouses instincts long ago forgotten – they are off hunting, anything that comes their way. Dachshunds are still used to hunt badgers in Germany, and are now very popular pets in America and Britain.

Right, the barkless Basenji.

Below, a Greyhound in full gallop during a race.

The best known is the greyhound, which is one of the most graceful animals in existence. There can surely be no one who has not seen several during a lifetime. Once used only for hunting or coursing, there are now a few people who breed greyhounds solely as show dogs. These differ from the working greyhound in that the emphasis is

placed on show points, whereas performance is the criterion by which the racing or coursing hound is judged.

They are graceful animals measuring from 26–31 inches at the shoulder. They are built for speed with long legs, plenty of heart room and very powerful muscles; and also have strong jaws in order to seize and kill on the run.

Greyhound racing was started in the United States when a stadium was built at Tucson in 1909, and other tracks sprang up within a few years. It was an American, Mr Charles Munn, who came to England and interested the late Brigadier-General A. C. Critchley in the sport, and the first British Stadium was opened at Belle Vue, Manchester in 1926. There are also a number of coursing clubs in Britain and regular meetings are held. Competition is keen, culminating with the best greyhounds in Britain running at Altcar for the Waterloo Cup – an event which has taken place every February since 1836.

It is said that the Saluki was first brought to England by the Crusaders, and there is no doubt that it was the hunting dog depicted in Egyptian tombs about 4000 BC. The breed is greatly loved by the Arabs who name it *El Hor*, the Noble One. A Saluki can be given as a present to an honoured friend but never sold and it is allowed the freedom of its master's tent – a liberty which would be unthought of with any other breed. The Saluki has always been used to hunt gazelle, sometimes in conjunction with a falcon which would sweep the desert far ahead and then hover over the quarry, thus giving direction to the keen sighted hounds.

They are very handsome and of greyhound conformation, with a short, smooth coat, and feathered ears, legs and tail.

The Borzoi is a powerful member of the greyhound family, which was bred to course wolves across the Russian steppes. Two hounds were employed for this dangerous sport, and they were trained to come up on either side of the wolf and hold him by the ears until the huntsmen arrived for the kill. They are one of the most elegant dogs in the world, with long, narrow heads, and dark fiery eyes.

But the giant of the greyhound clan is the Irish Wolfhound, which is never less than 31 inches tall. Rough haired and formidable, yet sweet tempered, this huge dog has the typical long head, punishing jaws, and tucked up loins of the greyhound. His coat is tough and waterpoof, and can be grey, brindle, white, black and any shade of fawn. The extermination of the wolf in Britain put him on the list of the unemployed but he has been used for hunting timber wolves in the

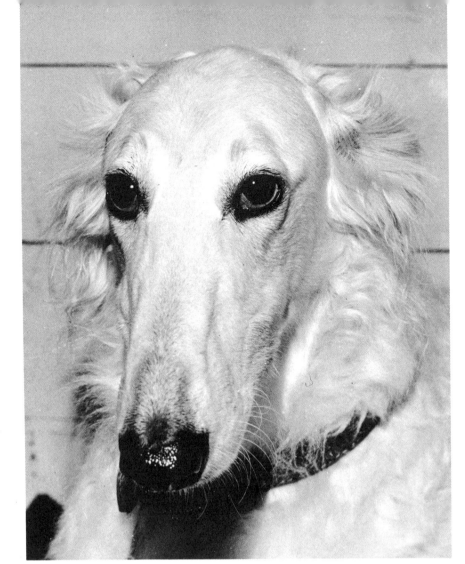

Left, Salukis are amongst the most beautiful breeds and are used to hunt gazelle in the desert. It is easy to forget that Salukis and Borzois and Afghans, all popular as house dogs in Britain and America, are very ancient hounds with exceptionally keen sight, capable of travelling long distances at great speed and of killing a deer, wolf or leopard at the end of the run.

Right, the elegant and aristocratic Borzoi.

Below, largest member of the Greyhound family, the Irish Wolfhound.

can be dark or light grey, yellow, red, red-fawn or brindle. Much admired by Sir Walter Scott, the breed has never failed to attract artists, and innumerable pictures have been painted showing this magnificent dog in every sort of sporting company.

The Afghans claim that the Afghan Hound was the dog taken into the Ark by Noah, and anyone interested in preserving their health is not advised to challenge this belief when in the company of Afghans! This shaggy, well trousered member of the greyhound family was brought to England around 1919 and first imported to the United States about 1926. It is well thought of in both countries and the principal dog shows never have any difficulty in filling the classes.

The Afghan Hound is a tall dog standing from 25–27 inches at the

Right, the Scottish Deerhound is only slightly smaller than the Irish Wolfhound, and like him is rarely, if ever, used for his original purpose.

Far right, two Whippets waiting to be judged at Crufts. They are still raced in both America and Britain, though it is not as popular as Greyhound racing.

United States. However, in both countries he has proved to be an excellent companion and a courageous guard dog.

The Scottish Deerhound is another handsome animal which was once used to hunt deer but which is now either purely and simply a show dog or the beloved companion of his owner. A very tall dog, he stands some 30 inches at the withers and is like a greyhound in appearance with a very thick, rough coat which

shoulder. It has an extremely fine and silky coat, the legs and ears being heavily feathered. A top-knot is a distinctive feature, as is the thin tail curving over the back. The Afghans have used him to hunt leopard and his large feet, muscular construction and thick coat are ideal for working in mountains where the going is rugged and the climate subject to extremes of heat and cold. The Afghan is a good example of how the members of the greyhound family have adapted themselves to their environment.

The Whippet cannot boast of a long and illustrious ancestry. A small greyhound in appearance, it was evolved by crossing a greyhound with a terrier; a dash of Italian Greyhound may have been added for good measure. It is an attractive little dog standing some $18\frac{1}{2}$ inches at the withers. The coat is smooth and can be brindle, fawn, black, white, blue, red or any mixture of these various colourings.

It was once raced extensively, principally in the north of England, and it was workers from England who first brought the Whippet to the United States. The dog is still raced in both countries – there are signs of a revival of interest in England – but it is now chiefly kept as a family pet and show dog. Sweet tempered, clean, and easy to groom and maintain, it is ideal for most purposes.

Top Favourites in America and Britain

These pages show the dogs that are most popular on both sides of the Atlantic, according to the numbers registered at the respective Kennel Clubs.

Above, Labradors . . . they are high on the list in Britain whether Golden or Black. Their intelligence, companionship and attractive looks make them in many people's eyes the ideal dogs to be called 'man's best friend'.

Below, the number one favourite in Britain and number two in America, Alsatians may well be the most popular breed in the world.

Top left, a Dachshund – all the intelligence and humour of these companionable little dogs is seen in this puppy.

Far left, a Shetland Sheepdog puppy.

Left, Poodles are still far and away the most popular dogs in America.

Top, a Cocker Spaniel with a beautiful shiny coat.

Centre, Chihuahuas are the smallest breed of dog in the world – and this minute puppy must surely be the smallest dog.

Above, who could resist this Beagle bitch? They are very popular in America in spite of the fact that they are working dogs by nature.

Above, Labradors were originally exclusively working dogs and many are still trained as gundogs, police and watchdogs, and as guide dogs for the blind. Here a black bitch does a spectacular jump over a fence having retrieved a shot bird.

Below, Miniature Schnauzers make lively and affectionate pets and are widely owned in America.

Centre, a beautiful Yorkshire Terrier all ready for the show. These dogs have been rising very rapidly in numbers in Britain over the last three years, and more and more are regularly finding their way into American homes. Despite their diminutive size and glorious, long silky coat they are true terriers in character.

Right, two beautiful and contented Alsatians – their amazing work as police and rescue dogs is described later in the book.

Far left, a magnificent quintet of Golden Retrievers covering four generations.

Left, Miniature Schnauzers.

Below left, three Rough Collies . . . these are the aristocratic and elegant cousins of the working collies and have not been used for herding sheep for many years.

Above, Yorkshire Terrier.

Above right, Cocker Spaniels.

Below right, Dachshunds.

Below, Yellow Labrador puppy.

The Toy Breeds

MARGARET SHELDON AND
BARBARA LOCKWOOD

It seems these days with Alsatians at the top of the popularity poll in Britain, that to be in the forefront of fashion one must own a large dog. And yet well over 27,000 toy dogs were registered at the English Kennel Club in 1970, and over 109,000 at the American Kennel Club. Perhaps this is not too surprising when one realizes that the Toy Breeds present a veritable ballet of colour and elegance. What dog lover would be unmoved by the glory of the pure white coat of the Maltese in contrast to its jet black nose and eyes; or by the long moustaches and steel coloured overlay on the shimmering coat of the Yorkshire terrier? Who could fail to be attracted by the bravery and haughty carriage of the Pekinese, whose lineage can be traced back almost as far as civilization itself? And who could ignore the Papillon whose outstanding beauty lies in his large butterfly ears and swirling tail?

There are fifteen breeds which are classified as Toys on the English Kennel Club register of accepted breeds, and are as follows:

Cavalier King Charles Spaniel
Chihuahua (Smooth coat)
Chihuahua (Long coat)
English Toy Terrier
Griffon
Italian Greyhound
Japanese
King Charles Spaniel
Maltese
Miniature Pinscher
Papillon
Pekinese
Pomeranian
Pug
Yorkshire Terrier

Over the last three years, Yorkshire Terriers have been first in popularity and numbers amongst the Toys in Britain, while Pekinese are second, with Cavalier King Charles Spaniels in third place. This does not include Toy Poodles which are not officially registered as a Toy breed.

The American Kennel Club recognizes eighteen Toy breeds and these differ just slightly from those on the English list. Six extra breeds are included: Affenpinscher, Manchester Terrier (toy) which is very similar to the English Toy Terrier, the Toy Poodle, Shih Tzu, and the Silky Terrier, and finally the English Toy Spaniel which is almost identical to the King Charles Spaniel. As yet the Cavalier King Charles Spaniel has not received recognition in America in spite of its tremendous popularity in Britain. The Toy Poodle and the Shih Tzu are listed in the Utility Group in England, while the only two breeds on the American Toy register which are not officially recognized at all in the English Kennel Club are the Affenpinscher and the Silky Terrier.

For the last two years Chihuahuas have been the most popular Toy dog in America, and they are sixth in the All Breeds list. As in Britain, Pekinese are second, and then come the Pomeranians, Yorkshire Terriers and Pugs. Poodles are also very popular, but cannot be placed as the registration number includes Large and Miniature poodles as well as the Toy dog.

There are a number of reasons why the Toy Breeds are so popular, one being the fact that these little dogs fit so easily into small modern houses and apartments. Another reason is that dog food has risen very considerably in price over the years, and most Toy Dogs need only three or four ounces of meat daily, whereas a Great Dane or a Saint Bernard eats three or four pounds.

There are, of course, crazes for various kinds of dogs which result in a particular breed galloping ahead in popularity. In Britain Toy Poodles were in fashion from 1958-1964 when they ceased to be quite so popular, although even now they are still in fourth place out of *all breeds* in popularity. Yorkshire Terriers then became the rage and have for some years now been sitting in third place in the All Breeds list and top of the Toy breeds. A sudden rise in popularity, however, is seldom good for the breed concerned, since it is difficult for the unscrupulous breeder to resist the temptation to satisfy the ever increasing demand for puppies at the expense of pure breeding. Faults may begin to appear, and there is a danger of unsoundness being stamped into a breed. It is very easy to breed in a

A Cavalier King Charles Spaniel, one of the largest of the Toy breeds and very popular as they are extremely friendly, attractive and lively family dogs.

73

fault but difficult to eradicate one, and it can take generations of selective and careful mating before the ideal is again achieved. For this reason great and sudden popularity is often feared by the serious and dedicated breeder. The fact that the popular breeds mentioned are not faulty or unsound is due to the hard work and careful attention to pure line breeding of the devoted breeders which has offset the machinations of those to whom money and sales are everything.

The Toy breeds are well represented in art, and many of the really ancient breeds are seen in pottery designs, tapestries, and of course paintings throughout the ages. A very detailed picture 'The Dog Market' painted by Abraham Hondius in 1677 portrays an incredible number of different breeds of dogs and includes many small Toy dogs. It is owned by an American dog lover Walter F. Goodman of Oyster Bay, New York.

Cavalier King Charles Spaniel
This lovely little dog was only recognized by the Kennel Club in 1945, and was a variety of the King Charles Spaniel until this year when it gained recognition as a breed on its own. However, this is not a 'new' breed: but rather a revival. 'Cavaliers' and 'Charlies' were one and the same thing under Elizabeth I and Charles II and appeared in a great many paintings of the old masters. As the years went by, many points in the spaniel's make-up altered and in the nineteenth century the King Charles Spaniel as it is now known came into being. The nose became flattened and as a result the dome of the head was rounded and a pronounced stop appeared between the eyes. Then an American gentleman at the 1926 Cruft's Show offered a large prize for the Best Dog and the Best Bitch which most nearly resembled the dogs in the paintings of King Charles II's reign. Interest was so great that a club came into

being in 1928 for this 'new' type of King Charles Spaniel, and in 1945, Cavalier King Charles Spaniels were declared eligible to compete for their own Challenge Certificates.

They are very sporting and active dogs, and are larger than most of the Toy breeds. The breed standard now lays down that the head must be almost flat between the ears, without any dome, and the stop shallow. The length from the tip of the nose to the base of the stop should be about one and a half inches, and it will be seen that the head structure of the Cavalier is completely different from that of the 'Charlie'. The ears must be set on high, and the whole picture should present a graceful and well balanced dog which is very gay and free in action.

A large number of these dogs are registered at the Kennel Club – currently there are over three thousand. The rise in popularity has been rapid and their numbers have almost doubled over the last seven years, and it is odd that they are not yet acknowledged as a separate breed in America since it was an American who was instrumental in bringing back this type in Britain.

Chihuahua

The Chihuahua originally came from Mexico and was said to have been bred by the Indians for use in many of their ritualistic ceremonies, and sad to say they were often eaten as tasty morsels at their banquets. Another theory is that the Aztecs, who were on the whole less barbaric and cruel than most of the Indian tribes, cremated them with their masters so that they might lead the way to eternal life. However, the Chihuahua, as we know him, was refound in Mexico in 1895 and is now acknowledged as the smallest breed of dog in the world.

There are two different types, the Smooth Coat and the Long Coat, and the breed standard is identical except in coat. They should be swift moving, alert, saucy and very small. The skull must be domed with a definite stop, and they should have very full, round and expressive, though not protruding eyes. The ears should be large, with good breadth between them. A special feature of the tail is that it should be furry and flattish in appearance, broadening slightly in the centre and tapering to a point.

The coat of the Chihuahua (Smooth coat) should be smooth, of soft texture, and close and glossy. The Chihuahua (Long Coat) as its name suggests has a long coat (never coarse or harsh to the touch) which is either flat or slightly wavy, but never tight and curly. There is feathering on the feet and legs, and an attractive ruff on the neck is an advantage. The tail must be long and fall as a plume.

English Toy Terrier

This diminutive breed used to be known as the Black and Tan Terrier (Miniature), and except that it is smaller, it is identical to the Manchester Terrier which is on the American list.

Most detailed advice is laid down in the breed standard as to tan

Two Chihuahuas, a Smooth Coat and a Long Coat. The miniature breeds have always had great appeal to men and Chihuahuas are the fifth most popular dog in America.

Left, a King Charles Spaniel.

markings. The tan must reach to the knees on forelegs, and there should be a sharp black line up each toe which is called 'pencilling', as well as a clear black thumb mark on the centre of each pastern and under the chin. The muzzle is tan up to the eyes and there must also be a tan spot on each cheek. While the hair inside the ear must be tan, tanning behind the ear is a fault, as are any white hairs or patches.

The head and muzzle should be long and narrow, and there is only the slightest trace of a stop. The ears should be slightly pointed and are likened in the breed standard to a candle flame in shape, and they must be erect by the age of nine months. The action of this little terrier should resemble the extended trot, and picking up the forelegs in a hackney action is quite incorrect. The tail is thick at the root and tapers to a fine point, and anything in the nature of a gay tail is undesirable.

English Toy Terrier breeders strive to keep this breed small without losing stamina and alertness, and an ideal weight is between six and eight pounds. Any signs of nervousness or timidity are wholly un-typical.

Griffon

This little dog can be said to suffer from split personality, for it can be haughty, disdainful, and bored; or gay, affectionate and devoted, according to mood. Most of them have beautiful manners, though they always do what they want and will never grovel for your favours – you grovel for theirs!

They were originally Belgian ratting dogs. The short haired variety is known as the Petit Brabançon, while the rough coated variety is the Bruxellois. They are an old breed and one appears in a painting by Jan Van Eyck dated 1434 which hangs in the National Gallery. In the late 1800's, Queen Henrietta Marie was very much taken with the Griffon, and in more modern times Queen Astrid of Belgium owned several.

Both varieties are identical except for their coats, and both types can appear in the same litter. The head should be round with a well pronounced stop and short muzzle. The ears should be really small and semi-erect, carried forward and not back, and the eyes are large and shining. In the United States the ears may be cropped, but of course in England this practice is illegal. The tail is docked short and is high set. In colour they may be red, black, or black and rich tan. The rough reds are the most numerous with the smooth reds coming next, followed by rough blacks. Smooth blacks are not much in favour and black and tans are seldom seen. The coat of the Bruxellois variety should be rough, harsh and wiry, and entirely free from any curl, while the Petit Brabançon has a short, smooth coat. The breed standard lists many faults, amongst which are a wry mouth, white patches of hair on the body, or a protruding tongue. It also censures the cutting of the coat with scissors, and the correct way to deal with the rough coated Griffon is to strip out the dead hair with the fingers twice a year, or when necessary. This is difficult and needs a certain amount of expertise. The beard is left really long with whiskers sticking out stiffly.

Right, a Griffon.

Below, a panoramic view of Crufts Dog Show.

Italian Greyhound

This is another dog, like the Toy Poodle, which has been bred from its large forebears to a miniature and yet retains the characteristics of the larger dog.

The designation 'Italian' is said to derive from the fact that the dwarfed greyhound was a great favourite of Italian ladies of fashion in the Middle Ages, and these dogs are often included in early Italian paintings. Queen Victoria was also greatly attached to these little dogs and kept several in her kennel.

The Italian variety is graceful, elegant and very typical of the racing greyhound in miniature. There is quite a variety of coat colour – fawn, white, cream, blue, black and white are all permissible, but tan markings on blue or black dogs are frowned upon, and so is any kind of brindle.

Japanese

This breed, contrary to its name, originated from China and was known at the same period as the Pekinese. It is believed that they gained the name of Japanese Spaniels because the Emperor of China presented one of these charming little dogs as a gift to the Mikado of Japan. They first arrived in Europe well over 100 years ago when a successive Chinese Emperor sent a breeding pair to the Emperor of Austria.

In general outline, the Japanese slightly resembles the Pekinese but is much longer in the leg. He has a lustrous and heavily feathered tail, well plumed over the back and flowing to one side. A quaint characteristic of this breed is that the white of the eye shows in the inner corners, giving the dog a look of astonishment (sometimes wrongly called a squint). The coat should be straight and silky and have no wave or curl, but there should be a distinct ruff at the neck. Several faults are listed in the standard of the breed, one being that the tongue must not show, and another that the tail should not droop. The ideal weight is around seven pounds.

An Italian Greyhound . . . a very ancient and supremely elegant breed.

King Charles Spaniel

These are really delightful little dogs, and were the companions of the ladies of the Court of Queen Elizabeth I, sometimes referred to as 'comforters' or 'gentle spaniels' as they were often kept under the voluminous skirts of the ladies to keep their feet warm. It has been said that they were used for another purpose which was far from pleasant, that of luring to their own bodies the fleas which the ladies harboured on their persons or which nested in their hair or wigs! They were great favourites of Charles II from whom they get their name, and Pepys, the diarist, is said to have been jealous of them for he felt the king spent too much time with them, and too little time on State Affairs. As we know, the spaniels in those days were much larger with long noses and flat heads, and were used as hunting spaniels.

The original King Charles Spaniel was black and tan, and was said to be evolved by the Duke of Norfolk; then the Blenheim appeared in the 1700's which was red and white and evolved by the Duke of Marlborough at Blenheim Palace. This was followed about the beginning of the nineteenth century by the Ruby which was a rich red colour, and finally the Tricolour Prince Charles which was black, white and red. It is laid down that both the 'Charlies' and the 'Cavaliers' of the Blenheim colouring should carry a wide, white blaze on the top of the head with a bright chestnut red spot or 'lozenge' in the centre.

The coat of the 'Charlie' must be long, silky and straight, with the legs, ears and tail profusely feathered. The eyes should be very large and dark with a sweet expression; the ears are low set and hang close to the cheek. The skull is large in comparison with the size of the dog, with a rounded dome and well defined stop, and the nose must be black with well defined nostrils. The ideal size is between eight and twelve pounds.

Below, a King Charles Spaniel, showing the domed head and pronounced stop, which differentiates them from the Cavalier.

Above, two Pekinese. One of the oldest breeds, Pekes only came to Europe in the middle of the last century and rapidly became extremely popular as they have the most delightful temperaments, aristocratic and independent, yet affectionate and loyal.

Right, a Japanese Spaniel, a longer-legged relative of the Pekinese with the same beautiful flowing coat and curly plumed tail.

Above, five young Pomeranians.

Right, A Papillon, or Butterfly Spaniel, so named because of its large, pointed ears, is one of the prettiest of the Toy Breeds.

Below, an Australian Silky Terrier, which is a cross between the Australian Terrier and the Yorkshire.

Maltese

There are many conflicting theories regarding the origin of the lovely white Maltese, but it is generally agreed that they belong to the original four French Toy breeds, and further back than that they are believed to have originated from a little town in Sicily called Melita. They were also popular in Ancient Greece and Rome, but in those days these dogs were minute, so small that they were carried about by Court ladies in the bosoms of their dresses. It is said that Landseer in the nineteenth century quickly included a Maltese in one of his paintings for he thought the breed was on the edge of extinction. Luckily the dogs have not disappeared and numbers have been slowly but steadily rising in Britain over the last seven years.

This little dog should not exceed a height of ten inches from the ground to the shoulder. The nose should be moderately long and pure black in colour, and from stop to centre of skull and from stop to tip of nose should be of equal measurement. The eyes should be dark with black eye rims. They are short coupled, cobby little dogs, with a profusely feathered tail arched over the back. The coat is silky, never woolly in texture, and should be quite straight and not too long, at any rate not long enough to impede free action. A brown nose or pink eye rims are bad faults and disqualify in the show ring.

The Maltese is a very brave and fearless dog, abounding in high spirits, needing a lot of affection and giving a great deal in return. Anyone who has owned one always falls for their intelligence and their sweet temperaments.

Below, the fairy-like White Maltese.

Left, a smiling and intelligent Miniature Pinscher.

Right, this attractive English Toy Terrier is earning his keep on the farm by collecting the eggs from the henhouses – but he is too small to carry the basket so the Great Dane comes to his rescue; an ideal working combination and the eggs are never broken.

Miniature Pinscher

This attractive dog hailed originally from the southern half of Germany, where in its larger form it was used extensively for ratting. It was also known in England in the Peat country, but these were standard size Pinschers and the 'Min Pin' was not really known in England until the 1960's, although a Miniature Pinscher Club was formed in Germany as early as 1895.

One of the most characteristic traits of this dapper little creature is his hackney action, and a sound, well moving 'Min Pin' is really a very pretty sight. It has a longish head and skull with very little cheek formation; the eyes are black, and the ears are set high and may be erect or dropped. The tail is docked and the coat should be smooth and shiny. Three colours are allowable – black, blue and chocolate, but all dogs must have the typical bright tan markings including the two spots above the eyes, and the black pencilling on the toes, but no thumb marks.

Papillon

This exotic dog is said to have hailed originally from Mexico along with other large eared small dogs such as the Mexican Hairless dog and the Chihuahua. More recently, however, they have been connected with Belgium, and are known, as their name implies, as the 'Butterfly Dog' because of their ears. The usual type of Papillon has prick ears, but there is a drop eared variety called Phalene or Moth, which is seldom, if ever, seen in Britain.

The breed standard lays down that the ears should be large with rounded tips, set towards the back of the head and far enough apart to show the slightly rounded shape of the skull. It is a fault for the ears to be semi-erect, as they must be one thing or the other. Another glory of the Papillon is the long, well feathered tail which arches over the back with fringes falling to each side to form the plume. It is a grave fault for the dog to have an unduly short or low set tail. The coat must be abundant, long, fine and silky with profuse frills on the chest and fully feathered forelegs and thighs. White is the predominant colour with patches of any colour but liver. When adult they are not unduly small, the ideal height at withers being eight to eleven inches.

The Papillon is one of the daintiest and prettiest of all the Toy Dogs, and in every way a most delightful companion with a sweet nature.

Pomeranians were originally descendants of large cattle dogs used for herding reindeer in Germany and they have featured as toy dogs a great deal in tapestries and embroidery and particularly in paintings.

Pekinese

This is undoubtedly one of the oldest breeds, although it is a comparative newcomer to England, since the first four Pekes were brought to this country in 1860, having been looted from the Imperial Palace in the uprising of Pekin. These handsome little dogs were known in China as 'Lion dogs' or 'Fo Dogs' and were bred to resemble a terrifying dragon in order to frighten away evil spirits. The ownership of these dogs was restricted entirely to those of royal blood and any commoner who acquired one of them was put to death. One of these blue-blooded members of the canine world was given to Queen Victoria, while the other three were kept by the Duke of Richmond who carefully raised this breed to be the forerunner of the magnificent Pekinese dog of today. One has only to own a Peke (or should we say 'be owned by a Peke') to realize what a really delightful temperament he has, for he is autocratic, independent to a degree and knows full well that he is royal and therefore superior to all other canines. Yet on the other hand he can behave like a clown with ears flying and tail swishing, happy to make you laugh *with* him – but if you laugh *at* him his royal dignity comes to the fore and he will immediately adopt a haughty mien.

In the mid-1950's this breed was highly popular in Britain and over

five thousand were registered, and although not quite so popular now, registrations are always around the four thousand mark.

The Pekinese is a dog with a massive head, wide and flat between the ears, and never domed. The muzzle is short and broad and the nose is well up between the eyes, with a deep stop. His eyes are one of his best features for they must be dark, lustrous and prominent. He has a lionlike mane around the shoulders, tapering to a marked waist. The top coat should be long and rather coarse with a thick undercoat and profuse feathering on ears, legs, thighs, tail and toes. Almost any colour is permissible except liver or albino.

The ideal weight is between eight and twelve pounds, the dogs being rather smaller than the bitches. There are some very tiny specimens known as 'Sleeve' Pekes, and while being extremely pretty they are often too small to breed from satisfactorily.

Pomeranian
As the name suggests, this dog originated in Pomerania in Germany and believe it or not, is a descendant of the cattle dogs and the animals used to round up reindeer. But of course the original Pomeranians were large dogs of the Wolf-Spitz variety which were the foundation stock of so many breeds such as the Elkhound, Samoyed, Keeshond and

Pugs have a reputation for being greedy and will do anything for food, but someone has taken it too literally and got this poor pug really worried . . . it would be wicked to leave any of this bone uneaten, but it is almost twice his size!

the little Schipperke of Holland.

Poms have appeared frequently in works of art; in embroidery, on brasses, in pottery, and particularly in paintings. Gainsborough was known to be interested in using the Pom as his subject and his painting 'Pomeranian and Puppy' in the National Gallery is delightful. Queen Victoria had a great love for this breed and her black Pom was said to be her favourite dog. She owned a kennel of Pomeranians which carried the Kennel Club prefix of 'Windsor'.

The head and nose of the Pom should be somewhat foxy and the skull large in comparison with the muzzle. The ears must be small and carried exactly like those of a fox. The tail is of great beauty in this breed having long, harsh, spreading hair, and is carried flat and straight along the back; the coat itself must be perfectly straight, and harsh in texture, and is particularly abundant round the neck, shoulders and chest, with profuse feathering on the thighs. Almost any whole colour is admissible and shaded sables are popular and should be shaded throughout with three or more colours, and with no patches of self colour.

Pug

Oddly enough, Pugs are said to have originated in Holland and the first pair were brought over from that country by William and Mary. Only three colours are permissible – black, golden fawn and silver fawn, and all dogs should have a black mask and black trace (line) along the backbone. The last type to reach England was the black, which came from China. They were extremely popular in Victorian and early Edwardian days, but after that popularity waned a little until

Cavalier King Charles Spaniel puppies.

the Duke and Duchess of Windsor took them up in a big way which gave a fillip to the breed.

As with all large headed breeds, such as Bulldogs, Pekinese and King Charles Spaniels, the Pug is not the most satisfactory of breeding pro-positions, and they have also gained the reputation in a few cases of being very indifferent mothers, hav-ing little interest in their puppies. It cannot be denied that Pugs snore, and this can be a drawback, as it is with many of the squashed nose breeds. He has, however, a delightfully affectionate nature, and is a loyal and devoted companion with a great sense of humour.

The Pug should be cobby and square and the head should be really massive with very pronounced deep wrinkles on the face. The eyes must be very dark and quite pro-minent, full of pleading and yet full of fire when excited. There is an oddity about the tail, for it is particularly attractive if it has a double curl or twist. The coat must be soft, short and very glossy. The blacker the mask the better, and the trace should extend from above the nape of the neck down to the twist. These dogs are not light-weights, weighing anything from fourteen to eighteen pounds.

The Pug has one failing – he is a real glutton. His soulful eyes gaze longingly at any little titbit of food, and no doubt he would leave his home for a chocolate drop or a piece of cheese. As a result he is prone to middle-aged spread and its atten-dant heart conditions. So be firm and keep him on a strict and inter-esting diet with very few carbo-hydrates.

The most popular Toy dogs of the day – two Champion Yorkshire Terriers and their puppy.

Yorkshire Terrier

The Yorkshire Terrier is certainly the most popular Toy Dog of the day, and more and more of these delightful little dogs are finding their way into the American show ring. For the past seven years they have headed the Toy Breeds registration tables in Britain with a yearly total rising from 5,531 to a current 11,016.

It is only partly true that the 'Yorkie' came exclusively from Yorkshire, and it is said that he has Scottish blood in his make-up. In spite of his diminutive size and trailing silky coat, he is a true terrier in every sense of the word. Some authorities say that he was bred originally from the old Scotch Terrier, while the Dandie Dinmont, the Skye and the Manchester Terriers have all been mentioned in connection with his evolution. They have only been bred true to type over the last hundred years in Great Britain.

His coat is his crowning glory for it must hang quite straight down each side of his body from a parting extending from the nose to the end of the tail. The falls from the head and on the chest are long, and of a rich golden tan; those from the back of the head to the root of the tail are of a dark steel blue. The ears should be erect, or semi-erect, and covered with short tan hair. When in the show ring his top knot is usually tied back with a narrow ribbon. His grooming and show preparation is indeed time absorbing and complicated, and while resting between shows the hair is usually kept rolled as a protection, since the coat normally trails the ground. The weight of this breed can be up to seven pounds.

The following breeds are recognized by the American Kennel Club only.

Affenpinscher

A tiny dog in stature weighing only about seven pounds and measuring about ten inches at the shoulder, but a breed which is extremely sturdy and has a great deal of courage. It came originally from Germany and was used primarily as a ratter. It is a shaggy little dog with a hard wiry coat, usually black in colour, a short docked tail, and high set, erect ears.

Silky Terrier

This is a modern breed evolved in Australia by crossing the Australian Terrier and the Yorkshire Terrier. The coat is glossy and fine but much shorter than that of the 'Yorkie', being at most five to six inches in length. The colouring is similar but the Silky Terrier is larger than the Yorkie and not as aggressive as the Australian Terrier.

There are two final breeds which are registered as Toy Breeds in the States, but are listed in the Utility Group in Britain, the Toy Poodle and the Shih Tzu, the latter is discussed at the end of the book.

The Toy Poodle

This diminutive breed was evolved by careful and selective breeding from the Miniature Poodle which in turn came down in size from the Standard Poodle. They have been recognized as a separate variety at the American Kennel Club since 1901, but only since 1957 by the English Kennel Club. They enjoy enormous popularity in both countries and from 1960 to 1964 they remained in second place in the All Breeds table in Britain with a huge registration total of over ten thousand a year, only being surpassed by their larger brother the Miniature Poodle. Both breeds have since dropped in numbers, though the Toy Poodle less than the Miniature.

The Toy Poodle must above all be active, intelligent and elegant. His eyes are dark and almond shaped; his ear leathers long, wide and low set, hanging close to the face, and his tail set fairly high, well carried, and never curled or turned over his back. As to colour, any solid colour is permitted, but parti-colours are looked on with distaste and are not acceptable in the ring. For showing in England the size must be under eleven inches at the shoulder, but in America the size limit is ten inches or under.

It is an expensive breed to own unless the owner is able to clip the

A sturdy and determined looking Affenpinscher, originally a German breed used for ratting, and recognized by the American Kennel Club only.

coat himself, which needs cutting approximately once a month. The art of show presentation is very intricate and needs years of practice, but the well groomed and trimmed poodle is a magnificent sight to behold. Most poodle owners will agree that once they have owned one, there is no other breed for them, since this marvellous little dog is above and beyond every other small breed.

It would appear that each Toy Dog in turn has something special to commend him to the enquiring new owner. The problem will be which to choose out of these many different breeds of little dogs. Obviously personal preference will be the guiding factor, backed up by the beauty of one breed set against the ease of grooming of another and so on.

In conclusion, it must be appreciated that ownership of a Toy Dog carries with it a certain amount of responsibility. These dogs are by no means delicate, but they are small and therefore they need protection. The intending Toy Dog owner must therefore be prepared to provide for his dog by giving protection against disease by means of inoculation and yearly booster injections; he must protect him against sudden attacks by larger dogs; and he must protect him as far as possible against accident. In addition every dog, whether he be large or small, has the right to expect clean and comfortable living conditions; properly balanced meals which are tasty, cleanly served and which give him the best possible nourishment; daily grooming (although he may tell you that he can do without that!) to keep his coat in good bloom and free from parasites; proper exercise in proportion to his size; and perhaps above all he has the right to expect love and affection from his owner at all times. In return, he is going to give a lifetime of loyalty, devotion and companionship. Surely not a bad return on the original investment?

Left, a Miniature Poodle with a beautiful show cut obviously complaining bitterly about having to go before the judges.

Right, a Miniature Smooth Haired Dachshund not classified as a Toy dog but about the same size and just as popular as most of them, if not more so.

94

Working Dogs

C. G. E. WIMHURST

A Husky. Sledge dogs are still vital to Eskimo life and are some of the hardest working dogs in the world. There are four main breeds of Northern dogs, though a lot of cross breeding has taken place and the term 'husky' is used generally for all sledge dogs.

A number of animals can be trained to perform useful work, but the dog is the only one which will willingly cooperate with humans and which can be trusted to use its own initiative when working away from direct control. For instance, sheepdogs often work sheep far away from the shepherd and yet drive the flock in the desired direction. Further, dogs show a pride in their work and are unhappy if they feel they have failed to gain the approval of their handler.

It is safe to assume that the first working dogs were the wolves from which all dogs have descended, and that they were hunters and guard dogs giving warning of the approach of enemies. Later, when men learned to farm, dogs were required to herd the cattle and flocks or sheep or goats and protect them from predators, rather than regard them as prey. This was not so difficult as it appears at first sight, since all training consists of bending natural instinct in the direction of useful work; wolves in Canada and in the United States have been observed to herd caribou in order to pick out the animals they had selected for the kill – just as sheepdogs separate certain sheep from the flock at the command of the

shepherd. Naturally, the instinct to kill would have to be curbed and our ancestors no doubt saw to this with a club. There was no sentiment whatever and working dogs were seldom kept as pets before the nineteenth century.

Hunting and herding were the two main occupations of the working dogs for many centuries, but when the sport of bull baiting developed dogs had to work to amuse a public more noted for brutality than kindness to animals. Chief among these dogs was the bulldog. Quite different from the show specimens we know today, which would be exhausted by any trial of strength, the old bulldog was a direct descendant of the English Bandog – a huge creature which existed in Britain before the Roman Conquest and which was later used by butchers to drive cattle to their yards. These dogs were entirely fearless and bull baiting became a popular sport and entertainment during the Middle Ages. Banned in the reign of James I, it was revived when Charles II was restored to the throne, and a special type of dog was evolved to make the spectacle even more entertaining. The only part of the bull which a dog could seize with any hope of throw-

97

ing or holding the animal was the nose, and so the bulldog was bred with a shorter face so that it could breathe while its strong jaws gripped the bull.

It was a cruel sport and the bull was baited over and over again. The unfortunate beast was tethered by the horns to a stake, and the owner of any dog was allowed to bait the bull upon payment of a fee. Sometimes the dog was tossed and killed, and the bull was often badly bitten about the nose. Quite frequently a bear was baited and the poor animal was led from town to town for this purpose and was one of the main attractions at Fairs.

Dog fights became popular after bull baiting was banned and the animals were expected to fight even when badly mauled. At first bulldogs were matched against each other, but they were found to be slow and cumbersome, so breeders began to introduce terrier blood with the result that two types of dog were evolved – one was the terrier which we now know as the Staffordshire Bull Terrier, and the other was the White Bull Terrier, which is sometimes called the White Cavalier. The latter became more of a show dog than a fighter but it should be noted that the modern bull terrier of both varieties is no longer a ferocious animal which attacks on sight, although neither will allow liberties to be taken by other dogs.

Another sport which was popular in the nineteenth century was located in the rat pits. Two Terriers would be matched against each other to see which could kill the greatest number of rats in a given time. One terrier was said to have killed 100 rats in five and a half minutes – one shake and the rat was dead. The miniature black and tan terrier was evolved by the working men of the North, who put the tiny animals in their pockets and so carried them to the rat pits, and their small size did not prevent them from killing rats as big as themselves.

Of all the dogs that did a job of work as opposed to providing entertainment, the turnspit dog was one of the hardest working, and did not go out of fashion until 1870. Said to be long in the body with short, bowed legs, a large head, and of various colours, the turnspit dog was put into a round cage which it

An illustration of the Ban-Dog; a vast creature known in England before the Roman Conquest.

Above, two Old English Sheepdogs, or Bobtails. They were the drovers' dogs in the Middle Ages and were also used for herding New Forest ponies, but they rarely worked sheep, and are now popular house dogs.

Right, a Scotch Collie. They are the most popular herding dogs in Britain and America and have been exported to many other parts of the world as well.

Right, a Springer Spaniel, having watched the shot bird fall to the ground, is waiting with every muscle tense for the command to go and retrieve it.

Below, a Border Collie, perhaps the most intelligent and hard working of all the sheepdogs.

turned in the manner of a squirrel at exercise. It was a treadmill from which there was no escape while cooking was in progress and one can only hope that the cook was kind enough to allow the dog to share the meal after his hours of duty.

It is now illegal to employ dogs to pull carts, but it was once no uncommon sight to see large dogs hauling light vehicles in France, Holland, Belgium and Switzerland. All kinds of loads were carried, although milk and bread were the most usual. The French and Belgian draught dogs, like their human masters, were called up for military service at the outbreak of the 1914-1918 war and performed useful work drawing machine guns, light ambulances, and other wagons.

They were large animals, usually of mixed breeding; strength and stamina being the most important requisites. St Bernards were sometimes harnessed to small carts in the Victorian era and used to give rides to children – a favourite subject of the early photographers. However, like horses, dogs have been long superseded by mechanical transport.

The pastoral dog is a member of a very ancient race. Sheepdogs were first used in Britain by the Brythonic Celts who owned great herds of cattle and thousands of sheep, although we do not know what kind of dog they used. Every country has bred a type suitable for local use, but one of the best known is the Scotch Collie which is the one most used in Britain and the United States, where the first specimens were introduced by the colonists, and has been exported to many parts of the world. The sheepdogs throughout the centuries were developed as the result of cross breeding between the Celtic dogs, the dogs brought into Britain by the Romans and, later, Anglo Saxon and Norman herding dogs, but the credit for the collie must be given to Scotland. It was known as early as the end of the sixteenth century and illustrations dating *circa* 1790 show a collie very much like the modern sheepdog. The breed spread down through England and Wales, mainly as a result of the Southern sheep farmers meeting the drovers who travelled most of the roads and tracks

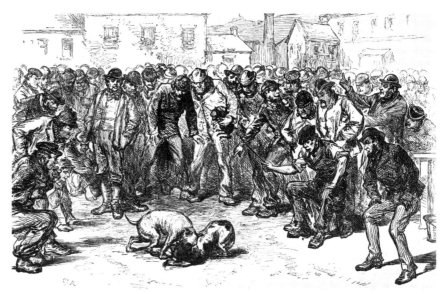

Early prints of dogs at work: top, bear baiting in the time of Queen Elizabeth was a popular sport and a regular feature at fairs. Bulls were often baited as well. Above, heavy bets were laid at dog fights which continued until the end of the last century. Bull Terriers were the breed most frequently used. Left, the wretched turnspit dog was expected to run inside his wheel until the joint was cooked.

Above, a Terrier provides entertainment by catching rats; sometimes the Miniature Black-and-Tan Terriers were used to kill rats as big as themselves. Centre, a dog cart used on a milk round. Below, Bulldog puppies; note the broad heads and squashed faces bred specially in the days of bullbaiting to enable the dog to attack and hold on to the bull.

between England and Scotland. The working collie must not be confused with the Rough or Smooth Collies which are now popular as pets or on the show benches. These were certainly bred from the working dogs originally but are rarely, if ever, seen to work sheep.

One of the supreme sheepdogs of the world is the dog popularly known as the Border Collie. There is no standard of points for this clever dog since there is considerable variation of size and type. Intelligence and ability to work with sheep are the most important requirements, and since the owner of a bitch naturally chooses the best dog available, collies over the generations have become one of the purest breeds in the British Isles. There are smooth and rough coated types, some are slightly built to enable them to cover hill country, while a heavier variety would be able to work on flat pastures without exhaustion– and a sheepdog must work all day from dawn to dusk.

The most important asset owned by a working collie is known as 'Eye'. This is the ability to command sheep by the power of the eye and it is not found in any other dogs. A collie can literally hold a sheep rooted to the spot by the hypnotic brilliance of its gaze.

A sheepdog starts training from six months of age onwards. It is not

true that a puppy is trained by allowing it to run with an experienced collie, and individual training by the shepherd is necessary – left to the older dog the pup would be more likely to pick up bad habits than useful instruction!

The sheepdogs of Hungary are hairy specimens of ancient origin specially bred to work long hours on the windswept plains of Hungary. The chief breeds are the Komondor, Puli and Kuvask, and specimens of each can be seen in Britain and the United States. The supreme sheepdog of Italy is the Maremma, a white dog of some 25 inches at the shoulder and resembling the Komondor, with which it shares a common ancestry.

The Briard of France is a big shaggy dog, while the Bouvier des Flandres stands 28 inches at the shoulder and is a cattle driving dog. The Germans think highly of the German Shepherd Dog, called the Alsatian in Britain, which is one of the oldest herding breeds in the world, and has the double job of working sheep with the shepherd and keeping the flock off the cultivated land. In Belgium, the three best known are the Groenendael, the Tervuren and the Malinois. All three resemble the German Shepherd Dog although there are important differences in structure when they are examined closely.

The Australian Kelpie, developed from the Welsh sheepdogs and collies taken to Australia by the first settlers, is a fine animal, and a slight infusion of Dingo blood is said to have given it added alertness. The Australian Cattle Dog is of medium

A White Bull Terrier. These dogs used to earn their living at dog fights, now they are house dogs and not at all ferocious unless provoked.

Above, Sheepdogs are indispensable to Australia's sheep industry and this Australian-bred Red Kelpie knows that the quickest way from one side of the crowded yard to the other is over the sheeps' backs.

Left, a Border Collie blocks a move by two sheep to escape by the power of his eye.

size and controls cattle by nipping at their heels. Another excellent worker is the Welsh Corgi which operates in the same way, sometimes called the 'Heeler' for this reason. There are two distinct types – the Cardigan with a long tail and the Pembroke with a very short tail. Both are well known, but the Pembroke is more often seen in Britain and the United States, where it has achieved a splendid reputation as a companion dog.

It would need a whole book to describe the sheepdogs of the world, but the subject must not be left without mention of the little Shetland Sheepdog. It is possible that the breed was originally descended from collies brought over to the islands, and gradually declined in size, since the sheep and cattle of the Shetland

Islands are also smaller than those on the mainland. The original working Sheltie has been refined until it is a perfect miniature of a Rough Collie but it is nevertheless a true little working dog.

Many villages in the Middle Ages kept a bloodhound to track down marauders and thieves, but the first real police dogs were recruited in 1859 by the Ghent police. These were so successful that the German authorities experimented with a kennel based in Brunswick, and other districts followed suit until, by 1910, the dogs were attached to all police forces on a permanent basis. The breeds used were German Shepherds (Alsatians), Dobermanns and Airedales, the latter being obtained from the famous Colonel Richardson of England. It is interesting to note that the three breeds are still used in the United States and Britain although the Alsatians are preferred by most police forces, as they are highly intelligent and can be trained to perform any kind of work physically possible for a dog.

Extensive use of the Alsatian in Britain and the United States developed after the First World War, when soldiers returning from the Continent brought back large numbers and began to train them in obedience, tracking and field work. It was not long before clubs were formed to train other suitable breeds as well as Alsatians, and now there is a network of associations in both countries which organize obedience competitions and field trials.

A trained police dog doubles the efficiency of the patrol man. All policemen are taught to observe closely but a dog has the added advantage of keener hearing and amazing powers of scent – senses which are not affected by darkness. It is obvious that a criminal has far less chance of escape once he has been detected by the dog. Furthermore, a policeman attacked by hooligans may be seriously injured if on his own – a dog will instil fear into his attackers and break up the mob until help arrives. Another important part of a policedog's training is tracking, and Alsatians and Dobermanns are efficient and quick workers and are scientifically trained to arrest a man without intentional injury. The dogs are taught to seize

An Australian Cattle Dog holding a group of Jersey cows at bay.

*Shetland Sheepdogs are perfect
miniatures of the Rough Collies, but
are nevertheless true working dogs.*

a man by the sleeve of his jacket, attempting to throw him off balance, and will hold onto an armed criminal even if they have been wounded. Police dogs are not always after criminals, they are employed frequently by security firms as guard dogs, and are used to find missing children, sick or aged persons and lost property.

Gundogs, sometimes known as Bird Dogs in the United States, are true working dogs, although their job is sporting rather than a run of the mill employment such as herding sheep. If a gundog could speak, he would certainly claim that there was no harder form of work than a day out with the guns.

They are bred specially for particular kinds or work, although in modern times, the work of one breed sometimes overlaps with that of another. Spaniels can be trained to do two jobs; first they search for and find game, flushing it from cover in front of the guns. Then they are expected to drop and await the command to retrieve the bird or animal which has just been shot, thus combining the job of retriever with that of pointing.

Only the Springer and the Cocker Spaniels are in general use. The Springer is one of the best all purpose gundogs, it quarters the ground with enthusiasm and retrieves well. Measuring 20 inches at the shoulder,

Right, Doberman Pinschers also make excellent police dogs, and are efficient at all kinds of work. They look very docile, but will become fierce and courageous on command.

Training an Alsatian in police work . . . the dogs are taught to arrest a man without intentional injury by seizing the sleeve of his jacket in an attempt to throw him off balance.

it has a thick, weather resistant coat and can be liver and white, black and white, and tan combined with any of these colours. The Welsh Springer is slightly different, being some three inches lower at the withers and his coat is invariably red and white. Like his English cousin, he is a splendid worker.

The Cocker Spaniel is a merry little dog and if bred from working parents is a hard worker and will search for game in the thickest cover, as well as retrieving quickly and willingly. There is a choice of colours and the coat can be black, golden red, roan, black and white, lemon and white, or any blending of these colours.

The Retriever is a specialist and is not expected to do anything else but retrieve. There are several varieties such as the Curly Coated Retriever whose coat is a mass of tight curls,

the Flat Coated Retriever of similar appearance but with a dense, flat coat, the Golden Retriever with a rich golden coat, and the Chesapeake Bay Retriever – an all-American production and a very good worker excelling in stamina and intelligence.

But the best known of all is the Labrador Retriever which can be yellow or black in colour. The ancestors of the breed were brought over from Newfoundland and landed at Poole in Dorset from the boats which brought over the cargoes of salted fish. The dogs have been considerably refined through careful breeding and are now very handsome animals. They will retrieve over any sort of terrain and through water, and will also do the work of a spaniel with equal efficiency. Intelligent and a good companion, the Labrador is the ideal dual purpose gundog.

Left, a Liver and White Springer Spaniel making a retrieve over a fence as one of the final stages of his training as a gun dog.

Below, a Champion Airedale Terrier. These dogs were some of the first police dogs, though they are rarely seen now since Alsatians are predominantly used in most countries.

Setters and Pointers, as their names imply, are trained to scent out birds and then freeze, pointing out, or 'setting' the direction of the game. Both breeds are still in use for grouse shooting on the moors and are frequently seen at Field Trials but, apart from these, there are not many sportsmen who shoot over them in this day and age.

There are three varieties of Setter – the English, Irish and the Gordon Setter. The English Setter is 25 inches at the shoulder and is a very handsome dog with a coat which can be blue and white, lemon and white, liver and white or tricolour with blue, tan and white.

The Irish Setter is very similar in appearance but higher on the leg and with a coat of shining rich chestnut. Very fast indeed, the Irishman is full of life and needs a firm hand in training.

The Gordon Setter is a black and tan dog which hails from Scotland. It is a heavier type than the other two, and a slower worker but very easy to train and persistent in the field. They have the reputation of being very much one-man dogs.

Pointers are very different in appearance from setters. Smooth coated, lemon and white, black and white, orange and white, self coloured or tricolour, the Pointer is an elegant dog though capable of hard work on the moors. Said to be of Spanish origin, it was once heavy

and slow and its present handsome lines are due to the introduction of Foxhound blood during the eighteenth century.

A service which no animal other than a dog can give to mankind is guiding the blind. A Guide Dog need not be of any particular breed provided it fulfils the necessary qualifications for size, intelligence and temperament, but once again it is the Alsatian which is used predominantly for this work. The successful employment of highly trained dogs during the First World War gave the Germans the idea that dogs could be taught to lead the blind, and after a certain amount of opposition, the idea took hold and the practice became widespread throughout the country. It took time for the movement to spread to the rest of Europe and the United States; and it was an American woman, Mrs Dorothy Harrison Eustace, who founded the first organization in Switzerland called L'Oeil qui Voit, or the Seeing Eye. Some time later she also established the first Guide Dog organization in America, after one of her dogs and his blind master had travelled over there from Switzerland and received great acclaim. Her establishments also inspired the first training school in Britain in 1933, and there are now training centres run by the Guide Dogs for the Blind Association in Exeter, Bolton, Leamington Spa and Forfar in Scotland.

Dogs of many breeds have been trained as Guides – Alsatians, Labradors, Golden Retrievers, and even a pure bred Malamute, while numbers of cross-bred bitches are taken in every year and give long and faithful service. The animals are obtained by gift, purchase, or are bred at the Centres, and it is their temperament that is all important. There must be no trace of nervousness, and the dog must be friendly, but not the type which fawns upon strangers. It must pay intelligent attention to the human voice, use its own initiative, and not show aggression towards other animals. Like Foxhounds, the puppies are 'walked' by volunteers from twelve weeks to ten months of age, and these temporary owners are expected to housetrain the pups, and familiarize them with traffic and riding in buses and trains. Training takes from four to six months and Guide Dog trainers are highly skilled and professional men and women who teach the dog to allow for the size of his master wherever they go, and to be aware of traffic. The dog is then matched to his prospective owner who must also be taught how to co-operate and care for the dog. This takes a month, by which time the two are usually perfectly in harmony physically and mentally for their new life.

There is no worthier cause and anyone having a little money to spare can be perfectly sure that a donation to the Guide Dogs for the Blind Association, no matter in what country, will be put to good use.

In all mountainous areas in the world dogs are employed to rescue people lost or hurt or buried in the snow after an avalanche. The Austrian Mountain Rescue Service is one of the most efficient and the breeds used are Alsatians and Belgian Sheepdogs, as both have the intelligence, stamina, and thick inner and outer coats necessary for working in Arctic conditions. Also, animals with dark coats are less vulnerable to the ultra-violet rays found at great heights which can affect their eyes. It is necessary to apply an anti-freeze mixture to their coats to avoid the snow sticking to the hair and thus hindering their work.

The men of the Avalanche Rescue Service must also be tough, experienced mountaineers with a thorough understanding of dog nature. Training of the puppies starts at twelve months with a grounding of general obedience, and is followed by jumping, both high and low, and the finding of objects hidden in long grass to encourage nose work. The dogs are worked over very rough ground and taken in every variety of transport so that nothing will be strange to them. The advanced training is very complicated and far too long to explain here. Briefly, the dog is taught to find first his master who is buried in a simulated grave of varying depths and at increasing distances away, and then a stranger in the same way, until he is ready for work in the snow. They find avalanche casualties by scent, and can detect victims buried under several feet of snow. Their work is invaluable, as men are

Good Dog! A successful retrieve through water. Labradors have very soft mouths and a well trained dog should leave no marks on the bird at all.

An English Setter out with the guns. They are sent ahead to find and put up the game for the guns following behind.

virtually helpless in such conditions.

The life of a Rescue Dog is hard and he is generally ready for retirement after eight years service. Some have been known to go on for much longer and Lupo, a member of the Tyrolean Service, saved many victims totally buried during his ten years of active service. Rescue dogs are also used to find people lost in the mountains or lying injured in places seldom visited by the people of the village.

Then there are the War Dogs of many breeds which have been used

throughout history. The Babylonians enlisted companies of fighting dogs as big as mastiffs, and when Julius Caesar carried out his invasions of Britain he was confronted with war dogs on both occasions. The Spartans fitted their dogs with iron spiked collars, and the war dogs of the middle ages were fitted with complete suits of armour. King Henry VIII sent a number of fighting dogs to Charles V of Spain who was delighted with their effect upon the enemy. Later still, Napoleon and Frederick the Great employed dogs as sentries and ammunition carriers.

But it was the Germans who really made full use of dogs in this way. Experiments were made during the Franco-Prussian War of 1870, and were so successful that a dog training establishment was formed for the sole purpose of training Army dogs. At the outbreak of war in 1914, the German Army had a force of 5,000 fully trained dogs to act as sentries, messengers, guards and ambulance dogs.

The French and Belgian armies also employed dogs as messengers and as draught animals hauling ammunition and machine guns. The Austrians thought highly of their war dogs and many Russian soldiers would have died from wounds had the ambulance dogs not found them in time. A war dog school was established in England in 1917 and the animals were mainly employed as messenger dogs. It is obvious that dogs had a better chance of crossing fire swept ground than a human soldier but there were many dog casualties in all armies in spite of their superior speed. The British war dog school was disbanded when the war ended and the French followed the British example.

The Germans however began to build up their war dog reserves. The Russians and the Japanese followed their example and the Japanese used thousands of dogs in their Pacific campaigns. A great number of trained war dogs were sent from Germany to Japan before Pearl Harbour and the entry of the United States into the war. The Americans were quick to see the value of dogs and over 20,000 were trained and used for all purposes, one of the most useful being the dog's ability to give advance warning of a hidden enemy when accompanying a patrol. They were used for this purpose for the first time since the Second World War by the troops in Vietnam. Another important service performed by dogs was mine detection. Many lives were saved by their ability to smell the mines buried under the battle fields. Ambulance dogs save men from death by guiding stretcher bearers

Below, an Alsatian of the Tyrolean Avalanche Rescue Service has found a buried victim and is digging to indicate the position. The work of these dogs is invaluable as they can find casualties so much quicker than men.

Below right, Belgian Sheepdogs are also used extensively by the Austrian Rescue Service since they have the necessary stamina and intelligence and the thick coat essential for working in arctic conditions.

Left, a Siberian Malamuk, perhaps the most handsome of all the Northern sledge dogs.

Below, a Labrador army dog finds an arms cache, which may have been in the ground for several months or even years. Nobody quite knows how the dogs achieve this, since one would think that all trace of scent would have been lost.

to the spot. These dogs are usually Labradors, who quarter the ground and then return and sit in front of their handler as a signal that they have found a casualty. Given the command, the dog then leads the way.

Guard dogs in all armies are usually Alsatians. The 'toughies' are trained to attack intruders in an active field of war, and they must be capable of handling and impeding the enemy until the arrival of the guard. The dog will only release at a command from his handler. Others are used for guarding a home base and are not trained to seize a trespasser, but only to prevent his escape until their handler arrives by threatening to attack.

Many Labradors have been trained to find caches of arms in enemy country, though no one quite knows how this is accomplished, since buried arms and ammunition have obviously been in the earth for months and even years, and one

A Samoyed and her two puppies.
These sledge dogs are the only ones
to have become really popular as
house dogs.

Above, a short rest for a team of sledge dogs in the Arctic.

Left, not much that an Alsatian cannot do . . . this trained guard dog will jump a seven foot fence and is here leaping through a flaming hoop.

would have thought that all trace of scent would be lost.

The sledge dogs of the North are one of the hardest working breeds, and are still essential to Eskimo life, although mechanical transport is being used more and more. The North could never have been opened up without the help of the huskies, and the fur traders and prospectors of America depended upon their dog teams for transport, as did, of course, the Polar explorers. In the past they were also used for hunting, and a pair of them would not hesitate to harass a polar bear until the hunters came up for the kill. Sledge dog racing is an increasingly popular sport in North America, the best known race being the Alaskan Dog Derby held over a 412 mile course.

The number of dogs in a team vary from four to twenty according to the load. Huskies can go all day

and sleep happily in the snow at night, their noses buried beneath the heavy hair of their bushy tails. A team will average four miles an hour, and a good team has been known to travel at twenty miles an hour for a short period.

There are four main breeds of sledge dog and the pure bred Northern dog is a beautiful creature; but much cross breeding took place with the rush of prospectors and Europeans northwards, and there are mongrels in many teams. The pure Eskimo dog, sometimes known as the Greenland dog, is a large animal with a wolf-like expression and there is no doubt that a number of wolfdog crosses were made.

The Malamute is also very handsome, and of ancient origin. The name is derived from the Innuit Indians, also known as Malamuts, who took great pains to preserve the purity of the breed. They have a broad skull, almond shaped eyes and a ruff round their necks. Sometimes the face has a black mask and a light coloured muzzle, and the combination is very striking indeed. About the same size as the Eskimo dog, the Malamute is strong and powerful and has served on many Polar explorations.

The Siberian Husky is the only Northern dog to have the word 'husky' as an official part of his name, though the word is used generally for all sledge dogs. They are smaller than the Malamutes or Eskimo Dogs with 'foxy' faces and very often striking blue eyes. Very popular in the United States where they are often kept as house dogs, they are also faster than other husky breeds and Siberian Husky teams have been very successful in winning the Alaskan sled races.

The Samoyed is a strong and graceful dog of great beauty with a very thick, stand off coat forming a ruff round the neck. The usual colours are white, biscuit and cream. The white is dazzling in effect and has a silver sheen not found on any other breed. Hailing from the Siberian Tundra, the dogs shared the tents of their masters, and were used for hunting, herding reindeer, and sledge work. They are very well known and popular house dogs in Britain and the United States.

The working dog has come a long way from the wolf-dog which hunted with our ancestors, and the end is not yet. New ways are being discovered for making use of man's oldest animal friend both in peace and war. In the fight against crime the police forces have struck a blow against the pedlars of drugs by training Labradors to seek out and find cannabis no matter where or how it is hidden. It is good to know that there is still a place for our dogs in spite of the mechanical and electronic marvels which are constantly being invented.

A contestant in a sledge dog race in North America urges on his team of Huskies.

New Breeds

WENDY BOORER

Every breed has its own distinctive characteristics, but how they were developed remains a mystery ... this handsome Chow has a black tongue ... why? ...

The enormous variety of shape, size, colouring and marking shown in all the breeds of dog that there are in the world, make it difficult to believe that there is a common ancestor behind them all. It is fascinating to speculate where all these differences came from and how each one became established as a characteristic peculiar to a certain breed. Why do Chows have black tongues? Why is it, when most puppies are born fully marked at birth, the spots on the Dalmatian only start to appear when the litter is two or three weeks old? Why, when many dogs have no dew-claws on their hind legs, do Pyrenean Mountain dogs (Great Pyrenees) have two? Breeds like these have been established so long that no one knows when these distinctive features occurred or how they became established.

Originally nearly all dogs were useful and bred specifically for the work they had to do. Because travelling was difficult and communications poor or non-existent, the sheepdogs in one part of the country could differ markedly in looks from animals doing the same job a couple of hundred miles away. Though looks and working ability are not necessarily closely connected, it is a natural assumption to link the two together. Thus all the vermin killing terriers of one Yorkshire dale would be black and tan while, further to the south, white dogs patched with black or brown would be doing the same job. Beyond stating that these early regional differences provided the basis for different breeds, we can say little more with certainty until we come to the nineteenth century when various new breeds were deliberately created and we know a little more about the methods used.

One such breed, deliberately created by one man, is the Sealyham Terrier. In 1850 a certain Captain Edwardes lived on an estate called Sealyham in Wales. He decided to improve the rather nondescript mongrel terriers used for bolting foxes and drawing badgers, and to produce a dog more uniform in type and unequalled in courage. New breeds cannot be created overnight and Captain Edwardes spent some 40 years breeding his terrier, testing the pups for gameness and disposing of those which did not measure up to his rather exacting requirements. He is believed to have used the wire Fox Terrier, which in those days was a working terrier with little resemblance to the barbered show ring terriers of today. To get the shortness of leg that would enable his dogs to go to ground easily, Captain Edwardes crossed in the Dandie Dinmont and possibly, at a later date, one of the white fighting Bull Terriers being produced in the Midlands was incorporated in the Sealyham's ancestry to add jaw power and tenacity. When the new breed first appeared in the show ring before the First World War they were still not very uniform in type, but rapidly improved in looks. This is one of the breeds with immense charm and a distinct sense of humour, but one must assume that these traits are a happy accident as they are scarcely one of the essentials Captain Edwardes was seeking to establish when he decided to create his little badger dog.

Another breed deliberately created by one man in the last century is the Dobermann Pinscher. About 1890 in Germany, Herr Dobermann started to breed what he believed would be a guard dog without equal. He used the Rottweiler and the old style German Pinscher. These early Dobermanns were rather thickset dogs and the elegance and refinement of the breed as it is today comes from a later cross with a Manchester Terrier and a black Greyhound. The breed is immensely popular in many parts of the world, particularly America, and because of this the original very suspicious, sharp temperament which was Herr Dobermann's ideal, has been to some extent diluted to make a more manageable animal in the show ring and a more suitable animal for a family pet.

It is extremely unlikely that any further breeds will be created, as were the Sealyham and the Dobermann, by the dedicated enthusiasm of one individual.

Since the first dog show was held in Britain in 1859, a complex machinery has arisen governing the show ring and pure bred dogs. In every part of the world where there

A pet Wire Fox Terrier probably has little resemblance to his ancestors which were working dogs and were used by Captain Edwards to create the Sealyham Terrier.

is an interest in pedigree animals, there is a Kennel Club maintaining a Stud Book which records registrations and supervises the way shows are run. The rules and regulations differ in each country but every Kennel Club maintains a list of breeds which it recognizes as pure bred and which will therefore be accepted in the show ring. The Kennel Club in Britain adds to its breed classification only those that are already officially recognized by overseas Kennel Clubs or that can prove by written records or pictures that they have been in existence and bred true to type for a century or more. In this way the deliberate creation of a new breed would not be officially encouraged. The American Kennel Club requires amongst other things that there should be over

300 specimens of a particular breed in the United States before it can receive official recognition.

The importance of the show ring to the survival of a breed should not be underestimated. The work for which many types of dogs were originally bred no longer exists. Dogs no longer turn spits to roast meat, nor do they pull bakery or milk carts and help to haul in fishermen's nets. They no longer drive herds of cattle long distances from farms to slaughter. Once their working function is superceded by machinery the kind of dog used for the job is liable to die out and there are a number of breeds which have vanished completely. Equally there are breeds which have been saved from extinction by dog breeders getting them officially recognized by

The Sealyham Terrier, created in the mid-nineteenth century as an efficient badger dog, has plenty of character and great charm.

Below, the Viszla is better known in America than in Britain, and is a game dog from the plains of Hungary.

Right, a peculiar characteristic of Dalmatians is that their spots do not appear until the puppies are two or three weeks old.

Pyrenean Mountain Dogs (Great Pyrenees) are spectacular and lovable dogs and are particularly good with children.

Below, Dandie Dinmont Terrier and family. This breed is also one of the ancestors of the Sealyham Terrier.

the Kennel Club and thereafter showing them. The publicity of the show ring will attract new adherents to the breed, either among other dog breeders or among pet owners who want something a little unusual. Similarly a newly imported foreign breed stands little chance of survival in its adopted country unless it is vigorously campaigned in the show ring.

What attracts people to new breeds? Some fall in love with a certain type of dog and never change their allegiance. Others like to pioneer something novel and as soon as it becomes well established will abandon it for something less popular. Some will hope that the rarity will enable them to make money by selling puppies at high prices.

Obviously what is new in one country may be well established in another. The following are a number of breeds which are new on one side

of the Atlantic or the other. Popularity is a gamble and only time will tell if they are going to flourish.

The Bearded Collie
This medium sized, very active, shaggy sheepdog has been used by Scottish farmers in the Highlands since at least the sixteenth century and probably longer than that. They had the job of collecting sheep off the moors and of driving cattle long distances, at a time when herds were moved on foot to market or slaughter. Close association with man over the centuries has resulted in an intelligent, devoted and responsive dog. Their working past means that they are animals with boundless energy which they retain until the end of their lives. The straight, harsh, weather resisting coat can be any shade of grey or brown with white collie markings. This breed was recognized by the English kennel club just after the

Second World War, since when it has become well established in Britain. Some hundreds have been imported into the United States where a very active breed club is campaigning for their recognition by the American Kennel Club.

The Lhasa Apso
This is one of four Tibetan breeds known in the Western world. Recognized in both America and Britain, this little watchdog has the long, harsh coat and the tail curled over the back which characterize most Tibetan breeds. The height should be 10 or 11 inches and the preferred colour of the coat is honey or golden. From this, and from their courage in defending their property, they get their nickname of Little Lion Dog. They are not numerous in Britain but are quite well established in the United States.

Above, a handsome group of Bearded Collies. This is an ancient breed which was used for herding sheep and cattle by Scottish farmers as far back as the sixteenth century, but was only recognized by the English Kennel Club after the Second World War and is still not recognized by the American Kennel Club.

Left, the Lhasa Apso has been nicknamed 'Little Lion Dog' because of its honey coloured coat and courage as a watchdog.

Right, the Dobermann Pinscher was created specially to be a guard dog without equal and was a rather thickset dog, unlike the modern Dobermanns which are more elegant and less suspicious by nature. They are very popular as pets as well as being one of the breeds used by police forces all over the world.

The Shih Tzu

Opinion is divided as to whether this breed originated in China or Tibet; the most likely assumption is that the Shih Tzu is the Chinese adaptation of the Lhasa Apso. Again the dog has a very profuse coat with a densely plumed tail falling over the back. All colours are found but a white blaze on the forehead and a white tip to the tail are desired points. The snub nose recalls other short-faced Chinese breeds, as does the air of comical arrogance. They were first seen in Britain in 1930 but made little progress until a few years ago when their soundness, liveliness and charm became more widely appreciated. Recognized by the American Kennel Club in 1970, they may take the United States by storm, as it seems unlikely that such a little dog, with such an air of its own importance, could fail to make an impression.

The Tibetan Spaniel

Spaniel seems a misnomer for these dogs which are often known as Tibetan Prayer Dogs. They have been known for centuries in the monasteries of Tibet where they are believed to have turned the Buddhist prayer wheels, and also acted as foot and sleeve warmers for the monks. A few of them reached Britain and America via India but only those in Britain have become recognized and well established. The Tibetan Spaniel, like the Shih Tzu, has a weight of between 9 and 16 pounds. They are alert, independent little dogs, rather reserved with strangers. The coat is silky and amply feathered. Most colours are acceptable but the most common are biscuit and sandy shades. Although reminiscent of a Pekinese, the Tibetan Spaniel is much less exaggerated in both shape and coat, having a moderately long muzzle and a comparatively long body.

Above, the Shih Tzu is recognized as a Toy Dog in the United States and is a most attractive and lively little dog that may well become very popular.

Below, a Tibetan Spaniel. They are rather like a Pekinese, though less exaggerated in both shape and coat.

Right, the Tibetan Terrier is very rare in the Western World but possibly the most numerous of the native breeds inside Tibet.

The Tibetan Terrier
Only a handful of these are registered yearly in Britain and they appear to be unknown in the United States. So far it is only in India that this breed has become well established. It was used by the nomadic tribes in Tibet as a herding dog and stands 14 to 16 inches at the shoulder. Like all Tibetan breeds it is both active and hardy and carries a long, fine, profuse coat which can be any colour except chocolate. Though possibly the most numerous of the native breeds inside Tibet, it is still a rarity in the Western world.

An Ibizan Hound.

The Vizsla
Rather surprisingly many continental breeds are better known in America than they are in Britain. This is certainly the case with the Hungarian Vizsla which is very popular in America and yet has only just begun to be shown in Britain. The breed was recognized in America in 1960 and has rapidly made its presence felt in field trial competitions and as a multi purpose gundog expected to find, point and retrieve game. Game birds and hares are plentiful on the plains of Hungary where this dog is believed to have originated some centuries ago as a companion to the war lords who used it for flushing birds for falconry.

Though the Vizsla is still valued in its native land two World Wars have depleted its numbers. Being essentially a pointer in type the Vizsla stands some 25 inches at the shoulder and has a tail docked moderately short. The coat is short and dense, without an undercoat, and is an attractive rusty gold in colour.

The Ibizan Hound
Paradoxically this new breed, which is unknown in America and only just getting a foothold in Britain, is probably one of the most ancient types of dog in existence. Certainly Egyptian frescoes of about the year 3000 BC show a dog of greyhound type with large upstanding ears very